Let Your Money
Work Harder for You

Let Your Money Work Harder for You

A Roadmap to Financial Security

JIM GENTILE

Cover design created by Bill Cole.
Cover idea and author photo by Jerri Gentile.
Cover arms compliments of Veronica & Patrick Dominguez.
Cover photo by Patty McNeill.

Library of Congress Control Number:		2013918685
ISBN:	Hardcover	978-1-4931-1708-6
	Softcover	978-1-4931-1707-9
	eBook	978-1-4931-1709-3

This book was printed in the United States of America.

Rev. date: 11/15/2013

To order additional copies of this book, contact:
Xlibris LLC
1-888-795-4274
www.Xlibris.com
Orders@Xlibris.com
142473

CONTENTS

Dedication vii
Foreword ix
Introduction xiii

PART ONE
Spendthrift versus Spend Drift   1

1   The Lottery: Change the Dream, Break the Cycle.......... 3
2   Automobiles: Lease or Buy? 11
3   Car Buying: Experience or Nightmare?...................... 19
4   Tax Refund: Spend or Save?....................................... 29
5   Insurance Is Not a Retirement Plan 33
6   Time-Shares: Vacations, Not Investments.................. 39

PART TWO
Home, (Not So) Sweet Home   43

7   Homes as Investments 45
8   The Refinance Trap.. 51
9   Strategic Defaults, Not So Strategic.......................... 57
10 The Reverse Mortgage Mistake 61

PART THREE
To Market, to Market, to Buy a Fat Pig   67

11 Knowledge Is Power, Get Smart Now 69
12 Real Rate of Return versus Simple Rate 75
13 Drive Fast, Build Wealth Slowly 83
14 The Rule of 72 and Why You Should Care................. 91

15   Calling a "Fowl" on Financial Black Swans 97
16   Trading Stocks Is a Mugs Game 107
17   Expenses Do Matter 115
18   Where to Invest Your Hard-Earned Money? 121

PART FOUR
The Gold at the End of the Rainbow   131

19   What's Your Net Worth Really Worth? 133
20   Who Needs to Be a Millionaire? 139
21   Getting Retired and Staying Retired 143
22   Putting It All Together, Improving the Bottom Line 155

Epilogue 163

Acknowledgments 167

Appendices

Appendix A (Chapter 12) 171
Appendix B (Chapter 14) 177
Appendix C (Chapter 15) 180
Appendix D (Chapter 18) 181
Appendix E (Chapter 22) 182
Appendix F (Chapter 22) 192
Appendix G (Chapter 22) 202
Appendix H (Chapter 22) 209

Dedication

I would like to dedicate this book to my Finance 101
professor at DePaul University in Chicago. After
failing to see eye-to-eye while taking the
class initially, I was invited back to
to try again. I took advantage
of the *mulligan* and aced
it a second time.
Thanks again.

Foreword

How often have you ever had the thought
if I only knew then what I know now?

That thought can apply to almost anything in our lives, but more often today relates to personal finances. Being married to Jim for more than thirty-five years, I have picked up some of the financial lingo and perspectives from someone who has been a numbers guy his whole life. Even after retirement, he continues to seek and study new financial information. Jim consistently creates or tweaks his spreadsheets covering the gamut of earnings to spending and everything between.

Since I have a background in accounting, finance is not my personal *Nightmare on Elm Street*. People who shy away from numbers think accounting and finance are the same. Yes, they're the same family, but much different relatives. Think of them as the drunk uncle and the prissy aunt; they may mingle at family functions but live in different worlds.

Everyone has done some basic accounting. Paying your bills and trying to budget your paycheck, for example. However, making that paycheck grow and support a future are the beginnings of finance.

There is not a "one shoe fits all" solution for peoples' finances. Everyone's financial goals will be different and continue to transform as they grow older and hopefully wiser. Don't buy into the theory only rich people need financial awareness, or that you are too young to worry about a fiscal strategy.

In writing this book, Jim provides financial ideas and logic for monetary novices in an easy-to-read format without their eyes glazing over from the first paragraph. Even if you consider yourself a savvy investor, some of the chapters may provide a different perspective or simply reacquaint you with some long-forgotten basics. It's like reviewing *The Rules of the Road*. Just because I have been driving for more than forty years, doesn't mean I remember all the details and follow the best policies. Not everyone will necessarily agree with all the content presented; that's okay. Questions, research, and an open dialogue should always be an important part of securing one's financial future. Past mistakes or missteps are part of the learning process.

I hope this book will provide you with:

1. Enough knowledge confirming that fiscal planning is not rocket science and often common sense.

2. The confidence in your ability to set and carry out some personal financial goals.
3. The knack to distinguish the difference between what will work for you, as opposed to only following some expert's plan of the month.
4. The desire to learn about more advanced strategies in pursuit of financial independence.
5. A promising economic future, so when you look back at your *then*, you will be satisfied with your *now*.

If nothing else, my husband Jim hopes that after reading this book if anyone ever asks you about your retirement strategy, you will *never* reply, "I'm waiting to win the lottery!"

JERRI GENTILE

Introduction

Here's an investment tip: Read *Let Your Money Work Harder for You: A Roadmap to Financial Security* and reap rewards afterward! Wow, I wish I could have read those words while pursuing my degree in finance from DePaul University in 1974. After earning a certificate in financial planning in 1991, my growing interest in personal finance was obvious. At this point, my knowledge base was instrumental in helping to create and run the first 401(k) plan for the Chicago Racing Mutuel Clerks Club. Having the option to retire at age fifty-five (2005), which I exercised, I now want to share my own insights with the reader.

This book provides choices on ways to begin planning a strategy for investment and savings. Each chapter points toward valuable research outlets and uses relatable examples to explain the mathematics behind the markets, investing, and compounding.

No matter your financial situation, it is chock full of valuable information about the unlimited choices in planning a savings strategy. What's addressed is the "who, what, when, where and why" of investing. It provides research data and presents easy to understand conclusions that apply to various life cycles, targeting all age groups or financial levels.

The book is divided into four sections. Each section contains chapters with similar focus about savings alternatives and financial strategies.

Part One: Spendthrift versus Spend Drift explores common expenses and how making simple adjustments can finally change the direction of your financial future. Part Two: Home, (Not So) Sweet Home examines some of the financial lures homeowners often face but may not understand. Part Three: To Market, to Market, to Buy a Fat Pig delves into the process of planning and carrying out a sound financial strategy and provides insight on investing alternatives. Part Four: The Gold at the End of the Rainbow explains the value of a financial plan regardless of income level.

If you are just realizing that Social Security cannot be relied on as a retirement plan, then this book is for you, and can help in mapping out a better financial future. Don't worry, you are not alone. I have a dozen nieces and nephews who fit this profile—they were my main motivation for writing this book.

The average individual starts later than some financial planners would recommend for securing a financial future. As the saying goes, "better late than never." My ideas are easily understood and can be put into place immediately and incrementally. So cast aside the misconception that only the wealthy can control their financial destiny. It's time for you to control yours.

Start now. With most everything in life, fundamentals are the starting point in following your goals and dreams. Here are some basic tools for building a financial foundation and explaining achievable results at various levels. It has worked for my wife and me, why not you too!

PART ONE

Spendthrift versus Spend Drift

Reviewing daily expenses can have a positive impact on
future wealth. Taking an in-depth look at your
spending habits and either altering or
eliminating specific items could
be the beginning of a more
secure financial future.

Chapter 1

The Lottery:
Change the Dream, Break the Cycle

On March 12, 2012, the Mega Millions jackpot reached a record high of $656 million. Three winning tickets split the jackpot. Mega Millions is sold in forty-three states. The Powerball, sold in forty-four states, changed its format on January 15, 2012, charging $2 a ticket instead of $1 and guaranteeing a $40 million annuity instead of a mere $20 million. These changes were made in order to increase the frequency of nine-figure jackpots. A Powerball spokesperson believed a $500 million jackpot was possible (it became a reality within the year), and the first one billion dollar jackpot in U.S. history could occur by 2022. The bigger the jackpots the more people play. The more people play the bigger the jackpots, a true self-fulfilling prophecy.

States rely more on revenues from measures that have a greater influence on poorer demographics. Taxes on cigarettes and alcohol disproportionately *affect* the poor: lotteries *target* the poor. None of this makes the economy any better. In fact, it impoverishes the underprivileged even more, making them dependent on the same entity profiting from their loss. *(http://the week.com/article/index/how the 500 million lottery is a tax on the poor)*

Most people understand the lottery, but with a take out of about 50%, it is the worst bet anyone could make besides playing Keno in Vegas. That does not stop intelligent individuals from taking part in or resisting the obvious gamble. According to Ben Shapiro, a columnist and author, households earning $13,000 a year spend about $1,170 annually ($22.50 a week) on lottery tickets, about 9% of their total income. As it turns out, many people are goaded into making poor financial decisions. How often have we heard "You can't win, if you don't play"?

Unfortunately, when playing the Powerball and Mega millions most of the money is front-end loaded into the big prize. If someone wins a smaller prize the winnings will most likely go toward buying another ticket. After all it's free money!

Why do people buy lottery tickets when odds are they will lose in the long run? I think we are paying for the dream. That's the period occurring between the time we buy the ticket and the time of the actual drawing, when reality eventually sets in. In that window, we imagine all those amazing things we would do with the money. We fantasize how the lottery cures all of our problems: financial, mental, and physical. We dream about how much we could help our relatives, our friends, and ourselves. How successfully can someone who has never had any financial wealth handle this newfound fortune? If the past holds any clues, then I would guess not very well. Here is a top ten list of depressing lottery stories. *(http://www.money.co.uk/ article/1002156-how-the-lives-of-10-lottery-millionaires- went-disasterously-wrong.htm)*

10. **Jack Whittaker**: This West Virginia businessman won $315 million in the Powerball lottery in 2002, the largest jackpot ever from a single ticket in American history at the time. While visiting a strip club Whittaker was robbed of $545,000 in cash and soon after Whittaker's granddaughter and daughter were found dead. Caesars Atlantic City casino sued Whittaker for bouncing $1.5 million worth of checks to cover gambling losses.

9. **Juan Rodriguez**: This New York City parking attendant was earning less than $30,000 in 2004 when he won $149 million in a Mega Millions drawing. Soon after taking the lump sum of $88 million, his wife filed for divorce and awarded half of his winnings.

8. **Billy Bob Harrell, Jr.**: This preacher working as a stock boy at Home Depot struck it rich in 1997, winning $31 million in Texas' lottery. Twenty months later, after divorcing his wife

and buying half-dozen homes for relatives, he committed suicide.

7. **Luke Pittard:** The man from Wales won a "measly" £1.3m (roughly $2.1 million) on the National Lottery. After the novelty had worn off and the lavish holiday, wedding and new home were done and dusted, he was bored and returned to work at McDonald's.

6. **Jeffrey Dampier:** In 1996, Dampier and his wife won $20 million in Illinois' lottery and used the money to buy relatives homes and to start a gourmet popcorn shop in Florida. Nine years later, Dampier was kidnapped and killed by his sister-in-law and her boyfriend who targeted him for money.

5. **William "Bud" Post:** In 1988, he won $16.2 million in the Pennsylvania lottery. He later described the experience as a *nightmare* and wishes it had never happened. Who can blame him after a former girlfriend eager to get her hands on the cash sued him, and his brother hired a "hit man" in the hope of inheriting the winnings. He invested in ill-fated family businesses and within a year was one million in debt. Today he gets by on Social Security payments.

4. **Mark Gardiner:** The man from London won £11 million (about $17 million) in 1995. Thirteen miserable years later, he still had some money, but he lost all his friends—even the one's he treated to new £100,000 homes—and lost touch with his family.

3. **Janite Lee:** She won $18 million in 1993. Her generosity in giving money to various political, educational and community causes was commendable, but eight years later she filed for bankruptcy.

2. **Michael Carroll:** He won a £9.7 million National Lottery jackpot in 2002. Since then he has appeared in court more than thirty times and been in jail for drug related offenses. In 2008, he admitted that only £500,000 of his windfall remained.

1. **An as-yet-unnamed Sicilian won £79 million on the Italian lottery in 2008.** Before he or she could even collect the winnings consumer groups were demanding the government seize the windfall. The winner has since gone into hiding, fearing the Mafia will pay a visit.

As seen in the list, lottery "losers" are not restricted to the United States. Nevertheless, a universal dream does not increase one's chances of making that dream a reality. The likelihood of winning a prize on the $2 Powerball drawing is almost 32 to 1 against a player. Winning $4 or doubling one's money is 1 out of 55 and the odds of winning the big one are 1 out of 175,223,510. That's right 175 million to one! Someone not only has to successfully buck those tremendous odds, but then must manage to be financially responsible with the winnings. That's a tall order. Lotteries, it seems, essentially target and encourage lower-income individuals into a cycle directly preventing them from improving their financial status. Is it possible to break the cycle?

We have covered the odds of making a lottery dream become reality and showed how big winners can become big losers. Now let us explore a way to crush the downward monetary cycle the lottery feeds. All one has to do is change the dream: modify the weekly "winning" time frame to a specific future date, accept a rational lower payout, and eliminate the appalling odds.

The lottery started in 1974, thirty-eight years ago. Consider someone with the foresight to *invest* $100-a-month instead of *dreaming* about the lottery. A $1,200-a-year investment into a growth mutual fund, reinvesting all the dividends would have grown to over $400,000 based on the S&P 500's actual returns (not the historical 10%). Since $65,000 is the average amount saved by people between the ages of fifty-five and sixty-four, this puts one well ahead of the crowd.

Why be shortsighted and continue to dream week after week about that big payout that never comes. Instead, a person should start to dream about the big picture they can control, their financial future. Transform the game, don't play, and instead invest. Changing the dream can break the cycle.

Full disclosure: I have bought lottery tickets in the past, personally and in groups at work (no one wants to be the one left behind). I never expected to win, and when I did, it wasn't much, $78 if I recall. I never spent more than $50 a year on lottery tickets, as I like to dream too, but only at $1 a week!

After I retired to Arizona I didn't buy a ticket for seven years until my sister visited, and the Powerball reached $500 million. After she left, I kept hearing her voice in my head: "You better buy a ticket, you can't win if you don't play." I couldn't stand the voices anymore so I "threw away" $20 on a quick pick, which won't happen again. The good news is that I was inspired to write the first chapter of this book.

Chapter 2

Automobiles:
Lease or Buy?

There has been much debate about the better choice, to lease or to buy an automobile. When making a *lease or buy* decision one must look not only at financial comparisons, but also at one's own priorities. What's important to the individual driver?

There are several items to consider before driving into the maze of car options. Think about the long-term commitment in ownership including increased repair costs as the car ages. Consider the higher monthly payments for the first few years turning into zero payments, depending on the length of ownership. The automobile industry is constantly updating their models. So, weigh the importance of the current gas savings, the newest styling to fit your needs, the latest technology, and the most recent safety equipment.

We now find out making a lease or buy decision is not so cut-and-dry. There are trade-offs, pluses and minuses, pros and cons to consider. Sometimes a *want* may even outweigh a *need*.

Buying and Leasing are Different

Car leases and purchase loans are just two different methods of *automobile financing.* Leasing finances the *use* of a vehicle; buying with a loan finances the *purchase* of a vehicle. Each has its own benefits and drawbacks. When buying, one pays for the entire cost of the car; regardless of how many miles driven or how long it's kept. Monthly payments are higher than for those leasing. One would make a down payment, pay sales taxes in cash or roll them into a loan and pay an interest rate determined by the loan company based on credit score. The first payment is made a month after a contract is signed. Later, there may be the decision to sell or trade the car for its depreciated value.

Leasing requires paying only a portion of a vehicle's cost, the part that is "used up" during the lease period. Sometimes the lessee has the option of not making a down payment, but there could be other fees and possibly a security deposit. The initial payment for the month ahead is made at the time a contract is signed. The automobile can either be returned at lease-end, or purchased for its depreciated value. There may also be an extra lease-end disposition fee, which is roughly $350.

If an individual uses a car for business purposes and gets the tax write-off, leasing has its advantages. But, if driving a new car every two or three years without the hassle of long-term maintenance has its appeal, then run the numbers and see exactly what that cost is over the long haul.

I pulled some figures from an advertisement for a 2013 midsized sedan with a manufacturer's suggested retail price (MSRP) of $23,270, tax included. Well-qualified customers could lease for no money down, pay $310 a month for 36 months for a total cost of $11,160. The lessee is responsible for maintenance, excess wear-and-tear, and up to twenty cents a mile over 12,000 miles. At the end of the lease, one can buy the car for $14,661. Since the lease is based on the MSRP, and no one should pay that (see Chapter 3), the cash investment is already too high.

The dealer's web site states the car's residual value after three years is 56%, if in good condition. That means according to their own calculation the car is worth only $13,031 ($23,270 x 56%), yet advertised at a purchase price of $14,661 or $1,630 more than the car's potential value. That's a 12.5% markup. By basing the lease payments on the sticker price (MSRP) then marking up the repurchase price, they are getting you "coming-and-going." Deal is not the word that comes to mind.

The lease offer in the example was the best I found advertised at the time, and included no down payment. For the chart on page 15, I used the vehicles' cost and made the following assumptions:

- The cars are not driven over the lease limits, or exceed the 12,000-mile limitation. This eliminates the twenty-cents-a-mile charge ($200 per 1,000 extra miles driven). In addition, no excessive wear-and-tear fees will be considered.
- All automobiles traded are in good condition garnering 30% of their original cost after seven years.
- All purchase loans are for three years and based on 3% annual percentage rate (APR).

These are just estimates used to simplify the twenty-one year lease versus buy scenario. On the ownership side of the example, all automobiles are held a minimum of seven years and kept in good condition for an above-average resale or trade value.

To keep the comparison chart on the next page as simple as possible, I only used the basic costs. Individual situations may vary and pricing can be higher or lower on the lease or purchase option. The chart compares the lease or buying costs of a midsize sedan priced at $23,270 representing an average car price.

Concentrate on the second column comparing the total lease cost to the buy and hold cost. The lease totals for twenty-one years are $78,120, plus a $350 disposition fee every three years ($2,450). Total lease costs are $80,570. With no incentive to buy your leased car (since it's marked up over $1,600) and no equity to protect, leasing becomes a *never-ending* car payment. The next four columns contain the cost of buying three cars of equal value every seven years, totaling $63,396. By keeping cars that long, there are payments in only nine out of the twenty-one years. Although paying more each month, the upside is no payments in twelve years. There is an expectation of one set of new tires on each auto and extra maintenance besides oil changes and tire rotations. These costs run around $1,500, based on my wife and I each owning three cars in twenty years. If a car was driven an average of 10,000 miles each year (70,000 miles) there is a possibility of trading it before it needs major repairs on drive trains or transmissions.

Total Auto Lease/Ownership Cost
Over a 21-Year Period

Seven 3 Year Leases	Lease Cost	Ownership	1st Car	2nd Car	3rd Car
		MSRP Price	$23,270	$23,270	$23,270
		Trade (30%)		$6,981	$6,981
		Loan Value	$23,270	$16,289	$16,289
Months (21 x 12)	252	**3-Year Loans (3%)**	36	36	36
Cost/Month	$310	**Cost/Month**	$682	$477	$477
Total 21 Year Lease Cost	$78,120	**Total Car Cost**	$24,552	$17,172	$17,172
Disposition Fee ($350 x 7)	$2,450	**Tires**	$500	$500	$500
		Maintenance	$1,000	$1,000	$1,000
		Total Cost to Own	$26,052	$18,672	$18,672
Total Cost to Lease		**Total Cost**			
Over 21 Years	$80,570	**3 Cars 21 years**	$63,396		
		21-Year Savings in Ownership	$17,174		

So what's the bottom line? In a twenty-one-year period, a buyer could potentially save over $17,000 if keeping each auto seven years before trading them in.

Again let's recap the variables of leasing versus ownership:

You should *lease* if: Driving a new car every two or three years fits into your lifestyle and you want lower monthly payments. You prefer a car with the latest safety features, technology, and one that's always under warranty. You don't like trading and or selling used cars and building ownership equity is not a concern. You drive an average number of miles, and are willing to pay more over the long haul for those benefits. You understand how leasing works and realize you will always have a car payment.

You should *buy* if: You don't mind higher monthly payments while building trade-in or resale value. You prefer the idea of having ownership of your car, paying off your loan, and being payment-free for a while. You take good care of your vehicles to keep down those unexpected costs on repairs after the warranty has expired. You drive more than the "average" miles and would rather drive your cars for more than three years to spread out the costs. You also feel the eventual total cash savings in ownership cancels the initial higher investment.

One final thought: If that new car smell is a major draw for you, car washes sell scented air fresheners that hang from a rearview mirror for a few bucks. Buy one every three years and pocket the extra $17,000.

Caveat: For simplification purposes on the chart on page 15, I used the MSRP price of $23,270 for both the lease and the auto loan. Both are negotiable. In the next chapter, I will discuss how to negotiate the lowest price on buying a new car.

Chapter 3

Car Buying:
Experience or Nightmare?

According to a January 2013 released Gallup poll, people who sell cars for a living are considered the least-honest, least-ethical professionals. They ranked below advertising executives, stockbrokers, HMO managers, and life insurance salespeople, even though the chief spokesperson for one of America's most widely advertised insurance companies is a lizard. They were also the only group to rank lower than the members of Congress. OUCH!

That being said, individuals who sell cars are not going to blow up one's retirement account, foreclose on someone's home, deny medical coverage, or shove the entire nation over a fiscal cliff. All a salesperson wants is to sell a car, it might be overpriced or a used piece of junk, but that's where "buyer beware" comes to the forefront.

The survey overlooks the fact there are honest and ethical people in every profession. My father sold cars in metropolitan Chicago for thirty years, starting with "Jim Moran, the Courtesy Man" in the late 1950s. He worked for one of the biggest Ford dealers in the city. He would sell 300 to 400 cars a year earning a slew of Top Hatter Awards, which he hung on the wall in our basement. Those awards went to the top salespeople. That's a lot of cars to sell and his secret was simple: No "hard sell" and don't gouge on the commission. He would make a little less on each car. The buyers were happy, would tell their friends about the deal, and Dad would sell more cars. Wash, rinse, repeat.

In the '60s, cars were reasonably priced. In 1966 my sister's new powder blue Mustang convertible cost $2,600. A Mustang today is over $30,000 or twelve times the price. The average salary has not increased that much in the same period. However, the car-buying experience has changed radically over the years. I remember the days when buyers got to select the exact options they wanted on their vehicle. They weren't forced to add an unwanted option to get the one they did. Today only a certain amount of cars are available at each dealership; salespeople are compelled to make the best deal for the dealership, not necessarily for the buyer.

I believe one of the actions that put car salespeople at the top of the *least-liked* Gallop poll is the *negotiation* dance, or the time spent going back-and-forth rehashing creative figures. It may also include the "I-gotta-make-a-living" scenario along with the subtle yet insulting innuendo that buyers don't know what they are doing.

Every dealership knows exactly what its bottom line is on any vehicle. Most dealers could sell a car under what's called a "house deal" and still make a decent profit. That was usually a contract for $200 over invoice, not MSRP, excluding taxes and some fees. The Internet has changed the playing field for purchasing a car. If a buyer is willing to do their homework, an enormous amount of information is available at one's fingertips. Anyone can find costs, comparisons, test-drive information and consumer comments. The following are a few tips to get one into the copilot seat of car negotiation.

Be aware of the biggest plum to the dealership, the dealer "holdback." This is where the manufacturer artificially inflates the "invoice price" (MSRP) 2% to 3%, refunding the money back to the dealer. This artificially inflates the dealership's vehicle cost. The dealer will not let go of the holdback. They are like a "pit bull on a pork chop" so don't even bring it up unless they are bold enough to say: "We are not making any money on the deal." On a $25,000 car, they may get back up to $750 from the manufacturer. The holdback allows the dealerships to advertise $1 over or under invoice and still make a profit.

Manufacturers provide several forms of financial assistance to dealers. Here are some discount options not readily advertised.

1. Advertising credits
2. Flooring assistance
3. Floor plan allowance
4. Transfer balance
5. Wholesale credits
6. Dealer cash, that which the buyer may be entitled to.

At "Edmunds.com," there is an application called "True Market Value" or the fair price that buyers in a specific area are paying for cars. TMV is normally less than sticker but more than invoice. It can be closer to sticker or possibly below invoice, depending on model popularity and excess inventory.

One of the newer hidden profits for the dealer is the documentation fee. That's a charge to do the paperwork and until 2002 it cost about $50. The new charge runs anywhere from $300 to $450 although the costs remains the same. It's pure profit for the dealership, similar to the holdback.

Dealers can write other fees into the contract and give these official sounding names like "S&H" or "Dealer Prep" or even "Shipping." These fees attempt to take added profit on the back end of the deal. Find out early what fees will be charged and negotiate accordingly. The manufacturer pays the dealer to remove the coatings and coverings protecting the vehicle so request a detailed explanation of the dealer's prep fee added to the price. This could just be an expensive car wash.

A good case can be made for buying last year's model, since they are often discounted to clear the floor for the current models. Buyers may not be able to get the colors they want or particular options, and end up paying more for a moon roof or leather interior that wasn't originally on their wish list. Those two options alone can cost $1,500 blowing out any savings depending on the deal. Buying a demonstrator—or demo—is another alternative. This "gently used" car is sometimes the previous year's model with low mileage on it. Consider that it has gained a full year of depreciation and lost one year's warranty, the mark down may not be enough to make up for those two factors.

Now it's time to talk about trading a vehicle. Kelley's Blue Book (kbb.com) gives an idea of what a specific automobile can be worth on a trade depending on condition. They rate cars in four categories:

Excellent—A price a dealer would rarely accept.

Very Good—A car would have to be in almost perfect shape to get this number.

Good—This is a possible negotiation point, depending on how much profit and commission is on the buying side of the deal.

Fair—This is the most likely bargaining position. Dealers may start the *dance* below this number.

When trading an auto in very good condition and in current demand, the dealer may be flexible knowing they can flip it at a profit with little added expense.

The percentage difference from fair to excellent can run around 20% on a trade. In most states, you only pay tax on the amount after the trade in. Example: On a $20,000 auto with an $8,000 trade, the state tax is calculated on $12,000, not $20,000, saving the buyer tax on the $8,000, or $720 at a 9% state tax rate. The dealer may remind the buyer of this savings as if it's theirs to give. Just keep in mind the savings was because of the buyer's asset, not the generosity of the dealership.

When selling a car outright instead of trading, make sure the tax savings is included in the asking price. It is much easier to trade in than to sell one's car, but that is a personal decision. The potential of making another 20%, minus the tax savings, might be worth the hassle. Usually the trade-in price is based on what you are going to buy. You will get a higher trade if the auto you are purchasing had a higher profit already built into the price. I suggest getting a quote on the car you will be purchasing without a trade. After basic negotiations, ask for a price with a trade. This will avoid paying more on the buy side and getting less on the trade side, all in the same deal.

Buying a used car is a different story. Forget the copilot seat of negotiation, the buyer is now flying blind and sitting behind the lavatory. There is no way to find out how much the dealer paid for the car in trade, or how much of an investment he made getting the car in selling shape. Make sure to deal with a reputable dealership to avoid hidden issues. Autotrader.com offers excellent resources for comparisons.

Whether someone is buying older or new, demo or used, often the timing can have an influence on the price. I have done some research on the best time to buy and get a good deal. Oddly, during a sale is not necessarily the answer. Some good times are:

- Near the end of the dealer incentive period because rebates are at their highest.
- At the end of the month. Dealerships tally monthly sales and try to meet targets, on which the salesperson may earn a bonus. A buyer who will help meet a target may get a better deal.
- In the middle of the week, when business is slow.
- Between August and October, depending on make and model, dealers are trying to clear the decks for next year's new ones, and there are unreported dealer incentives in the form of percentage increases in holdbacks.

Be aware that when looking for a specific car, by waiting too long, the current year's models (or specific trim levels or colors) may run out. This creates a supply-and-demand imbalance that can cancel any savings. Also, keep in mind the car's depreciation in the first year or two. As soon as the next year's models arrive, this "new" car is worth even less.

Some dealers offer a free oil change when bringing a car in for a trade-in estimate. Take advantage of those free oil changes as a starting point for getting a car's potential value. However, it is not a good idea to go in for the free oil change and walk out with a new car unless one has done all the research first and negotiated the best deal possible.

The auto market is always changing and prices rise and fall rapidly, therefore it's important to shop around. When car buyers are prepared and know the numbers behind the deal, this can make them formidable negotiators.

True Life Example

In the year 2000, Lexus came out with the RX300. The car was a big seller and in demand from the start. My wife was looking for a midsized SUV and fell in love with the Lexus. We went for a test drive, but priced at over $40,000 with no discount, it was simply too much money. We decided to wait a couple of years hoping the demand would ease with other newer models available. Instead, with our car budget we took this opportunity to pay down our home mortgage.

In December 2002 Lexus had their annual Christmas sale. Remember the one where they put the big red bow on the car? I know from my dad being in the business all dealers are slow between Thanksgiving and year-end. That was a good time to buy.

My wife had a significant birthday on the horizon, so we went to a local Lexus dealership to negotiate her gift. The sticker price on the model with the options she wanted was $41,389 (MSRP) and they agreed to discount the car $5,689 to $35,700. After adding in destination, title, and taxes, we paid $38,300 "out the door." That was a lot of money to spend on a car, but we intended on keeping it at least ten years. (I have excluded the trade-in savings and tax benefit we received to set apart the true value of the car.)

Flash forward to May 2012 when I finally convinced my wife to sell her baby with 62,500 miles on it. Let's run the numbers and see what it cost to drive her Lexus RX300 over that 10½-year period. What's added to the purchase price of $38,300, are the following maintenance and service costs.

- One set of Tires—$600
- 30,000-mile service—$750
- 45,000-mile service—$550
- Brakes and wheel bearing—$500
- One new battery—$100 (the original lasted eight years)

The cost to own and drive the Lexus over 10½ years was $40,800. Amazingly, we discovered the car was still worth $10,750 on a trade, 28% of its original purchase price. Subtracting the $10,750 from the driving cost of $40,800 (maintenance included) the actual cost of the car over that period was $30,050 or $2,862 a year ($238 a month).

The cost to lease a new Lexus RX300 over the same ten-year period was $499 a month, or around $6,000 a year. Multiplied by 10½ years and the total lease cost is $63,000. The difference between owning the Lexus RX300 and leasing a new one every three years is $32,950 ($63,000 minus $30,050). I did the math, now you do the math.

Chapter 4

Tax Refund:
Spend or Save?

In the first quarter of 2012, the Internal Revenue Service cut checks totaling $212.8 billion to 75.3 million taxpayers, with each check averaging around $2,860. Similar figures also applied to the first quarter of 2011.

With the Fiscal Cliff looming into 2013, Paul Cherecwich, Jr., chairman of the IRS Oversight Board stated that more than sixty million taxpayers might have to wait until March or later to file their returns. Waiting on those refunds would cause a noticeable hit to consumer spending in the first quarter. That explains the mind-set of the average consumer.

Let's take a close look at the tax refund process. First, taxpayers give the government a tax-free loan of around $55 a week for a year ($2,860÷52). Next, they have to fill out numerous forms and wait up to two months the following year to get the money back with no accrued interest. So thrilled to get a refund they cannot wait to go out and spend it, bragging to friends and neighbors about the size of the check as if they just won the Lotto.

Now I don't want to kick a dead horse. However, did I mention it was *our own money?* Let me try to explain why I consider this whole tax refund a losing proposition for the average taxpayer. At the beginning of the year, I approach my hypothetical friend and neighbor, Bob, with a financial brainstorm. I try to convince Bob to give me that same $55 a week. I tell him the following year I will return his $2,860, but only after he fills out the proper paperwork sometime between February and April. Oh, and by the way, he will need to wait up to an additional six weeks after the paperwork for receipt of his money. What do you think Bob would hypothetically tell me to do?

After Bob settles down, I explain that I am doing him a huge favor by keeping his money safe and out of his "grubby hands." After all, it is a forced savings plan and he should be ecstatic I am willing to help him. When he inquires about any interest on his money, I tell him that's my fee for keeping his money safe. I assure him he will be delighted when I refund that big check for $2,860 the following year. After screaming, "But it's my money," Bob storms off, never to speak to me again.

Warning: This was only a hypothetical scenario; I do not recommend trying this with real family, friends, or neighbors.

So, why do more than seventy-five million taxpayers routinely give the government free money for up to fifteen months? The forced savings explanation is the answer most offered when asked. I would believe that argument if the refund money were invested into an Individual Retirement Account (IRA) or other saving vehicle the following year. However, is this really a savings plan or just a delayed spending plan? According to the IRS Oversight Board, consumers are spending their refunds.

Now, I think it would be wiser for the "taxpaying forced saver" to have $55 immediately put to work in an IRA. By the time the government refunds the original $2,860, that $55 each week could have grown to $3,692, using an 8% return on stocks. After ten years, the accumulated $28,600 in refunds might grow into $43,274 in savings.

Over a longer thirty-year period, saving nothing more than $55 a week in an IRA, or $85,800, could grow to over $343,000. That's the magic of tax-deferred compounding. Your money is making money. An added bonus, the government offers a tax break on your savings. Depending on one's tax bracket, up to 28% or $800 is returnable in the form of an extra tax deduction.

The beauty of an IRA is threefold:

1. Deferral of investment earnings and taxes over long periods.
2. The tax deduction received from a total IRA contribution is at the taxpayer's highest bracket level, giving the biggest bang for the buck.

3. The tax on the IRA's future withdrawal will conceivably be at a lower tax bracket, maybe as low as 10%.

The downside is the taxpayer does not get to spend his or her tax refund every year while locking it up in an IRA until age 59½. This is not a bad thing, but rather a step in planning a financial future. I believe this is the genuine forced savings plan. Instead of just working for your money, it works for you.

Chapter 5

Insurance Is Not a Retirement Plan

Term is a form of life insurance that is pure protection based on a mortality table. People can buy it for periods of one to thirty years. All other policies, including whole life, universal, and variable, are pure protection with cash value added. Insurance agents like to call these policies retirement plans, because a portion of each month's premium is invested for one's future retirement.

Insurance policies purchased through a salesperson include a payment to the seller. This money comes right off the top of the policy owner's first payment. Agents who sell whole life insurance policies earn about 55% of the first year's premium with the agency getting about 40%, leaving only 5% of the owner's premium for investment. The next nine years the takeout is 10% of the premium, split evenly between the selling agent and the agency.

These policies come with high fees, deducting as much as three percentage points from the annual return. It's often impossible to tell what the return on the investment will be, or how much is going toward the insurance and the investment portion. Most policies, by design, don't start to build decent cash value until their twelfth to fifteenth year. Cashing in after ten years could cost a chunk of money. Surrendering the policy in the first five years will result in expensive short-term insurance with almost zero payout.

Premiums for term insurance are economical for people in good health up to about age fifty. After that, premiums start to get progressively more expensive. The same holds true for whole life policies, though people who need coverage starting in their sixties and beyond may have no alternative. Many companies will not sell term policies to people nearing or beyond age sixty-five.

In the early 1980s, Universal Life Policies were quite the rage with interest rates at 12.5%. I looked at my old policy bought in May 1981. With an initial deposit of $2,000 and annual premiums of $960, my $100,000 policy was projecting a cash value of $191,572 by age sixty-two. The estimated estate value (on death) after thirty-one years was $291,572 ($191,572 + $100,000), assuming the interest rate never fluctuated from the initial 12.5%. My total cost over that period would be $30,800, producing a return of 9.15% plus the insurance.

Why not cash in the policy after thirty years, buy simple term insurance, and pocket the difference? Sounds like a great idea. I knew people who were buying universal life policies as a substitute for retirement plans. Insurance agents must have been salivating like Pavlov's dog.

Unfortunately, buried deep in the plan's policy was a *guaranteed* rate of return of only 4%. By law that's the rate the insurance agency was required to pay. A mere 4%, when the initial teaser rate was over 12%. If rates eventually dropped down to the guaranteed rate after my purchase, thirty years later the cash value would be zero and my entire premium would go toward the cost of insurance. Even though that did not happen, the policy's cash value peaked in my middle fifties. I recognized the warning signs and decided to cash out before lower interest rates and higher cost of insurance started to take their toll on the bottom line.

There are better ways to save for retirement. Looking back, I could have invested differently. A better choice, for me, would have been to buy a thirty-year level term policy in 1982, paying about $130 a year to lock in a $100,000 pure death benefit. That frees up $1,870 the first year and $830 the following years to be invested into an IRA, compounding tax-deferred. Based on the S&P 500's real rate of return for the period, over $114,000 would have accumulated after thirty years. That's more than the original universal life's death benefit, and no one has to die to collect. See the table on the following page.

Year	Starting Balance	Real Rate of Return	Income	Total	Next Year's Investment
1982	$1,870	8.11%	$152	$2,022	$830
1983	$2,852	8.11%	$231	$3,083	$830
1984	$3,913	8.11%	$317	$4,230	$830
1985	$5,060	8.11%	$410	$5,471	$830
1986	$6,301	8.11%	$511	$6,812	$830
1987	$7,642	8.11%	$620	$8,261	$830
1988	$9,091	8.11%	$737	$9,829	$830
1989	$10,659	8.11%	$864	$11,523	$830
1990	$12,353	8.11%	$1,002	$13,355	$830
1991	$14,185	8.11%	$1,150	$15,335	$830
1992	$16,165	8.11%	$1,311	$17,476	$830
1993	$18,306	8.11%	$1,485	$19,791	$830
1994	$20,621	8.11%	$1,672	$22,293	$830
1995	$23,123	8.11%	$1,875	$24,999	$830
1996	$25,829	8.11%	$2,095	$27,923	$830
1997	$28,753	8.11%	$2,332	$31,085	$830
1998	$31,915	8.11%	$2,588	$34,504	$830
1999	$35,334	8.11%	$2,866	$38,199	$830
2000	$39,029	8.11%	$3,165	$42,194	$830
2001	$43,024	8.11%	$3,489	$46,514	$830
2002	$47,344	8.11%	$3,840	$51,183	$830
2003	$52,013	8.11%	$4,218	$56,232	$830
2004	$57,062	8.11%	$4,628	$61,689	$830
2005	$62,519	8.11%	$5,070	$67,590	$830
2006	$68,420	8.11%	$5,549	$73,968	$830
2007	$74,798	8.11%	$6,066	$80,864	$830
2008	$81,694	8.11%	$6,625	$88,320	$830
2009	$89,150	8.11%	$7,230	$96,380	$830
2010	$97,210	8.11%	$7,884	$105,094	$830
2011	$105,924	8.11%	$8,590	**$114,514**	

Married couples, especially those with a family, need some insurance to fill the gap in their younger years. Term insurance can be a real bargain for a family who has not yet acquired a *living estate* (a respectable net worth). Once achieved, there is no longer a need for life insurance, unless someone prefers to pass on his or her entire estate intact.

One final point to consider: Warren Buffett, the famed chairman and CEO of Berkshire Hathaway Inc., had no fewer than six insurance companies in his portfolio in 2011. This suggests that there is more money in owning stock in insurance companies than buying the investment products they sell.

Chapter 6

Time-Shares:
Vacations, Not Investments

The main goal of an investment is to make money for the investor. Doing some research, I discovered the average time-share owner will not make any money and has only a slight possibility of breaking even. In my early twenties, I went to my first time-share presentation in the Chicago area offering $20 for one hour of my time. It turned into an unpleasant experience when a few people remained and the hard sell began.

Flash forward thirty some years when I won a time-share for a week in Sedona, Arizona. My wife and I voluntarily sat through a presentation offering two train tickets, valued at $120, for a tour we already were planning on taking.

We visited three different time-share presentations during the trip. Each offered different types of property. The first one was a converted mobile home community and the presentation was low-key with zero pressure to buy. The second was newer and beautiful, but the presentation reminded us of an inquisition, especially when they brought in their closer for the kill. By the third round we were jaded, answering the questions in a way they knew there would be no sale. We ended with $300 in cash and gifts, and a stern warning not to come back until we were serious about buying. There were more incentives offered to close a deal on the spot, which included cash and a "free" cruise.

We were amazed at the never-ending amount of *incentives* available and decided to do some research when we got home. On average, a one-week time-share cost $10,000 to $14,000 to buy. The markup is roughly 50%, which pays for the marketing and sales costs. When someone buys a $12,000 time-share, they would be lucky to sell it the next day for $6,000. It takes five years to lose that same 50% in a new automobile, another depreciating asset. If avid travelers have their hearts set on a time-share, the best way to make the purchase is in the aftermarket from the original owners.

The time-share pitch is standard. First off, it's not just one hour, but as long as it takes to make a sale. Potential buyers are queried about their credit, income, and assets. And, by the way, did you bring a check? The original friendly chat now turns into a background check, a bit like being vetted by Homeland Security.

Remember the least-liked car salespeople; they could get a few tips from a time-share rep.

The next step includes creative accounting regarding travel habits and expenses. This manipulated estimate then makes the original cost of $10,000 seem like a bargain spread over a lifetime of travel.

What they don't talk about are the costs in maintenance fees averaging somewhere between $500 and $800 each year. According to the American Resort Development Association, in 2010 average annual maintenance fees cost $731. Experts believe the costs are still rising. No real effort is made to remind the buyer that this $10K to $14K buy is *only* about the cost of a room. There are no estimates tossed around for airfare, gas, food, and entertainment, which are a huge part of vacation travel.

Let's consider how long it takes to break even on a $12,000 time-share. This scenario is, based on buying in cash, use of a room one week each year, and a $650 annual maintenance fee. After fifteen years, the total is $21,750. If we can find an equal vacation rental for $200 per day or $1,400 per week for the same fifteen years, we will spend $21,000, that's the breakeven point.

This example excludes any potential interest on a financed purchase, any special assessments for building repairs, and eventual increases in maintenance fees. Also excluded is any earned interest lost on the money invested and maybe finding similar lodging for less than $200 a night.

If someone did finance the cost through a time-share company, costs could run twice the regular mortgage rate. I wonder how many individuals walked away from their *investments* after being underwater during 2008–2013. In many bankruptcies, trustees will eventually have to dispose of a time-share. In fact, the resale of time-shares in economic failure is so prevalent that a trustee once joked that owning a time-share was a precondition for filing bankruptcy. That speaks volumes about a time-share being an investment.

Executive producer at RedWeek.com said, "Very few time-shares increase in value." Florida has even considered passing a law that would make it illegal to mention the phrase "investment opportunity" in a time-share sales pitch. Anyone considering a property investment should keep in mind the purchase of a second home. Time-shares are not real estate investments, but rather investments in a lifestyle.

PART TWO

Home, (Not So) Sweet Home

A house is often one of the largest and most significant
purchases people make. The initial decision to
buy may not be the only financial dilemma
homeowners will face. Home ownership
and finance will regularly cross into
areas where pitfalls and promises
must be thoroughly
investigated.

Chapter 7

Homes as Investments

M ost homes were a terrific investment for California homeowners retiring anytime between 2000 and 2005. With record sale profits, they could cash out and buy two houses in Nevada or Arizona. Some were buying small homes in the Las Vegas area and using them as weekend getaways. Other parts of the country didn't fare nearly as well when the high point came in 2006.

Some would argue a best-case scenario is a home provides a roof over your head, keeping you protected from the rising and falling prices of the rental market. A not-so-rosy situation and it turns into a money pit. This can create the illusion of money well spent. Despite what the entire real estate industry would have people believe, not everyone should own a home.

Research from Robert Schiller, the Yale economist, shows that since the year 1900 home prices have gone sideways or even declined for long periods. In fact, except for two steep run-ups, one after World War II and the other in the late 1990s, real estate has not been the winning investment every one claims it to be. The last seven years have proven real estate can go down, and go down fast, as millions of people learned the hard way.

The run-up in home prices from 1997 to 2006 was 9.7% on average and 7.1% in real returns. In addition, from 2000 through 2006, the figures were 11% and 8.2%. That's an unsustainable increase in housing for such a short period. Knowledge of the historical evidence would have led to the conclusion that prices don't go straight up. In fact, in just the period between 1972 and 1984, the U.S. had experienced three boom-bust cycles in housing prices: 1972, 1978, and 1984. Also in the early 1990s, home prices in Orange County California dropped about 60%.

Looking at the longer-term data, we also see a different picture. For the period 1890 through 2005, inflation-adjusted home prices rose just 103% or less than 1% a year. I can imagine fewer investors would have piled into the residential home market if fully aware of the historical evidence. By October 2011, the Case-Shiller Composite (twenty largest cities) home price index dropped 31%. It seems like people conveniently forgot the lessons of the last four collapses:

1. Texas oil collapse of 1986. By July, oil prices collapsed to $10 a barrel, with drilling dropping to the Great Depression levels.
2. The real estate and stock market crash in Japan in the late '80s. Neither market has fully recovered *twenty-five years later.*
3. The collapse of Gold from the late 1970s through early 2000s. Gold came back in the last ten years, but the total return over the thirty-year period had been minuscule, even with the recent run-up.
4. The NASDAQ's crash of 2000 sent the averages from over 5,000 to around 1,000, an 80% decline. The Index today is still 26% off the peak *thirteen years later.*

Homebuyers made the mistake of comparing simple returns on infrequent real estate transactions. Let's assume a home in 2005 sold for ten times the original price in 1950. While that produces a simple return of 900%, the real (inflation-adjusted) annualized return was less than 1%. I remember when we sold our parents' home in 2003 for $245,000. They originally paid $24,000 in 1954, resulting in a tenfold increase. However, decisions based on such evidence means falling prey to the mistake of *recency bias*, which is the tendency to give too much weight to recent experience while ignoring long-term evidence.

Another likely error made by homebuyers is not realizing the simple rate of return ignores all the costs of residential real estate. That figure includes significant transaction costs, closing costs, property taxes, maintenance, and improvement costs. An assumption of 1% for maintenance costs alone would yield a real return of below zero.

Now in defense of home ownership—my wife and I have owned three different residencies in thirty-six years—people need to live somewhere. Often it's said, a man's "home is his castle" and I would not trade the experiences owning any of our homes. My wife and I were lucky enough to have in-laws and friends who helped us with many rehab projects, cutting the costs of ownership way down. In addition, there is a great feeling of achievement when able to complete a home project.

A house is an asset that should appear on the balance sheet with the mortgage. As it's paid off (a forced savings plan), it adds to one's net worth. Another plus in the great feelings column is paying off a home loan. Don't ever believe any financial wizard that would recommend borrowing against one's home and investing the money in the stock market. That was a so-called great "strategy" in the late '90s and we saw how well it turned out in the 2000–2003 market decline. In the 2008–2009 crash, people lost not only on their homes but in the stock market too, a double whammy for those who thought leveraging a house to the markets was a great plan.

No one should ever invest without understanding the nature of the risks involved. It's also important to avoid the mistake of recency bias, which leads to buying yesterday's winners (typically at higher prices) and selling today's losers (typically at lower prices). To avoid that error, make sure to research the historical evidence.

As Spanish philosopher George Santayana famously remarked, "Those who cannot remember the past are condemned to repeat it."

Chapter 8

The Refinance Trap

My wife and I bought our first home together, a townhouse located in Hanover Park, IL, in 1978. Six years later, we were ready to move up to something bigger without common walls and a larger yard. In the fall of 1984, we found a home in Addison, IL, for $105,000 (about $40 per square foot). That was cheap compared to the today's current average of around $100 per square foot. The bad news: the cost of borrowing was at a time when interest rates were 13.5% for a fifteen-year loan and over 15% for the thirty-year term. We opted for the shorter loan so we would be able to have the house paid off by 1999.

We took out a $70,000 loan with $3,209 in closing costs and a payment of $909 a month. With 20%

down, we didn't have to pay PMI (private mortgage insurance) and we could pay our own property taxes and insurance. Escrow companies can be inept at withholding enough money to cover taxes and insurance. We've heard horror stories of homeowners getting refunds after too much was withheld one year followed by a collection notice seeking twice the money back the following year. Most individuals could do a much better job of budgeting for and controlling their own account.

As the years went by since our home purchase, the mortgage rates started to come down. At the time, the pros recommended that if rates dropped 2% from the original loan it was "wise" to refinance. The mortgage experts claimed that lower monthly payments were enough to make up for the added closing costs, saving money in the end. Not being one to doubt the "experts," we took the bull by the horns and refinanced three times over the next ten years, down to 7%. Our payments went down every time and once we even took out an extra $10,000 for home improvements. What no one stresses is every time a home is refinanced the same old fees apply:

- Title Insurance: $320
- Document fee: $200
- Underwriting fee: $200
- Loan Origination fee: $195
- Settlement or Closing fee: $195
- Recording fee: $55

- New Survey: $500 (avoided if an old survey is still in good standing).

In the 1980s, *points* on the new loan were also an added cost. These ran up to 3% of the amount borrowed, which were expensive. With so many hands in the proverbial pocket, there was little or no room for homeowners. In our situation, we took solace in the so-called fact that in the long haul the lower payments would eventually make up for the entire short-term expenses incurred. A few years into our final refinance in 1993, a new fifteen-year loan, we decided to prepay an extra $500 a month toward the principal balance to accelerate the loan payoff.

In the fall of 1999, with our original fifteen-year loan set to expire, reality set in. We still had six years left on the loan and even with the extra payments made; our payoff balance was still around $32,000. I added up all the "savings" from the lower monthly payments plus the cash we took out and the total was still short of our current payout balance. Adding in all the expenses we paid to refinance, it looked like the only people making any money were those refinancing the loans. How could this be?

Home loans are structured in such a way that more interest is paid in the early years, with smaller amounts going toward principal. In the later years, the opposite is true. Every time someone refinances, the clock resets and again more goes to interest while simultaneously adding to the number of years until payoff. Not many people refinance an initial thirty-year mortgage after seven years with a new twenty-three-year mortgage. Our original fifteen-year loan turned into a thirty-year mortgage, not saving us what I had originally calculated.

The following chart explains a thirty-year $200,000 mortgage loan taken out at rate of 4.25%. The principal and interest payments are $984 per month. For this example, the borrowers put down more than 20% and chose not to set up an escrow account, wisely budgeting for taxes and insurance on their own. After the first year, the payments total $11,808 of which $3,373 went to reduce the principal and $8,435 went toward interest. That's a difference of $5,062 more paid out in interest. Fourteen years later 62% of the payment or $100,720 went toward servicing the debt (interest). Only $61,640 paid down the principal. It takes until 06/01/2027, before one-half of the original $984 payment, or $492 goes toward the principal.

The thirty-year totals at the bottom of the table show how much interest is paid on the loan, an astounding $154,240. Total payments were $354,240 on the original $200,000 borrowed. A whopping 43% went toward interest, and 65% ($100,000) was paid in the first fourteen years. Like Bill Murray in *Groundhog Day*, constant refinancing creates a mortgage time loop.

Loan Amount	$200,000	Term	30 Years	Interest Rate	4.25%
P&I Payment	$984	Total	Total	% Toward	
Month/Year	Payment	Principal	Interest	Interest	Balance
10/1/13	$984	$276	$708	71.95%	$199,724
10/1/14	$11,808	$3,373	$8,435	71.43%	$196,627
10/1/15	$23,616	$6,892	$16,724	70.82%	$193,108
10/1/16	$35,424	$9,893	$25,531	72.07%	$190,107
10/1/17	$47,232	$13,738	$33,494	70.91%	$186,262
10/1/18	$59,040	$17,749	$41,291	69.94%	$182,251
10/1/19	$70,848	$21,933	$48,915	69.04%	$178,067
10/1/20	$82,656	$26,299	$56,357	68.18%	$173,701
10/1/21	$94,464	$30,854	$63,610	67.34%	$169,146
10/1/22	$106,272	$35,607	$70,665	66.49%	$164,393
10/1/23	$118,080	$40,565	$77,515	65.65%	$159,435
10/1/24	$129,888	$45,738	$84,150	64.79%	$154,262
10/1/25	$141,696	$51,136	$90,560	63.91%	$148,864
10/1/26	$153,504	$56,767	$96,737	63.02%	$143,233
6/1/27	$162,360	$61,640	$100,720	62.03%	$138,360
30 Year Totals	$354,240	$200,000	$154,240		
06/01/27	$984	$492	$492		

These three choices tilt refinancing in the borrower's favor:

1. If deciding to refinance a thirty-year loan after five years, take out the new loan for only twenty-five years, if possible. The payoff date of the loan will remain the same with lower payments, but not as low as the original loan.
2. Shop around to get the lowest fees and *do not* roll them into the mortgage. Borrowing the money to pay the fees over thirty years is never cost effective.

3. Rolling additional borrowed funds for personal use into the refinanced mortgage is not a sound financial decision. Even at today's low interest rates of 4.25% a $20,000 *cash out* added to a thirty-year loan costs over $15,000 in interest. A five-year home improvement loan at 5% would only cost $2,645 in interest.

Even if able to get a new loan with minimal fees, the key to refinancing is what's eventually done with the extra savings from the lower monthly payments. If it's added to an IRA or put into a 401(k) that's another step toward financial independence. Using the savings for nonessential items adds unnecessary years and costs to the mortgage. When a lower monthly payment is necessary to prevent a foreclosure, be sure to understand all alternatives and outcomes. The sooner one gets out of debt, the better off they are.

The bottom line: The decision to refinance is not always just financial, but also personal.

Chapter 9

Strategic Defaults, Not So Strategic

Strategic default is a borrower's decision to stop paying on a debt, despite the financial capacity to make payments. This is usually associated with residential and commercial mortgages. Defaults occur after a substantial drop in a property's value results in a debt owed that is greater than the purchase value. The property has negative equity (known as "underwater") and is expected to remain so in the future. This activity picked up following the bursting of the real estate bubble. Strategically defaulting on a home mortgage was nicknamed "jingle mail." Owners walk away and mail the keys back to the bank.

After the borrower decides to stop paying, they can still live (free of the costs of payment or rent) in the home until the lender forecloses, which could take anywhere from several months to years. The borrower may use this time to pay off or negotiate other debt. Some people pay lawyers to drag out the fated foreclosure even longer for half the cost of what rent elsewhere would be.

Mortgage lenders may negotiate with defaulting borrowers to assure maintenance and occupancy of the property until the lender can take title and market the house. Some allow greater time than the law requires (3 days) to vacate the premises. They may even agree to pay a fee to the defaulter if the home is left in excellent condition. A study in September 2009 from the credit-reporting agency Experian and consulting outfit Oliver Wyman estimated close to one fifth of troubled mortgages in the U.S. involved borrowers who were strategically defaulting.

The law does not provide much incentive to stay put. Thirty-nine states allow a lender to come after a borrower's other assets and income if in default. In the eleven states that do not allow this practice, the restriction applies only to original home loans used to buy property, not to home-equity lines of credit. There is some legal confusion about mortgages issued to refinance existing mortgages. Nevertheless, lenders rarely slap borrowers with a deficiency judgment. The procedure is costly and usually not worth the expense because of the limited assets most Americans own aside from their homes.

The tax code does not impede people from defaulting strategically. Until recently, people had to pay taxes on any foregone debt. If someone walked away from a house worth $100,000 less than the amount owed to the bank, the money forgiven was essentially income, and the debtor had to pay tax on it. However, in December 2007, Congress made mortgage debt cancellation nontaxable for personal residences (extended in 2012). Congress's aim was to facilitate the renegotiation of underwater mortgages, but the move had an unintended result: reducing the cost of walking away.

Even without any social and moral considerations, there are several economic reasons not to default. First, if the interest on the mortgage is less than renting an alternative house, it's to the homeowner's advantage in delaying the default. Second, walking away from the home involves relocation costs. Third, defaulting on a mortgage ruins people's credit ratings, causing negative consequences on their future ability to borrow. Fourth, if the mortgage is a recourse-loan, the borrowers face the risk of losing any assets they might have if the lender files a deficiency judgment.

Other things to consider, such as moving costs and transfer expenses, are irreversible expenses. With uncertain housing prices, the option to wait is more valuable because the higher the volatility of home prices, the higher the expectations of recovery. Many of the hard hit areas in Phoenix, Las Vegas, and Florida have recently showed a strong housing rebound. Those who thought they were doing right by "strategically defaulting" years ago might now be surprised to find out had they held on they might now be above water. In addition, rent costs skyrocket as people turn to renting in lieu of ownership, creating a shortage of decent properties. Finally, the property owner is not as generous as the government; if you don't pay you are gone.

The more people walk away from their homes, the more houses are auctioned off, further depressing real estate prices. This additional decline can push more homeowners into negative territory, leading to still more defaults. At that point, strategic default without social stigma is just another viable financial option. Every time a borrower defaults, it makes future mortgages more expensive because lenders have to cover those costs. The higher cost and reduced availability of credit depresses home prices even more, jeopardizing the possibility of an economic recovery. This is why the housing recovery took so long to hit bottom.

Some significant barriers to strategic default are both moral and social. People who consider strategic defaults immoral are less likely to use it as an option, while people who know someone who defaulted are more likely to regard this financial choice. The social pressure not to default is weakened when homeowners live in areas with high frequency of foreclosures or know other people who defaulted strategically.

There are many stories about people who default on their homes. Often job loss or a serious medical condition makes default the only recourse. These cases involve individuals drained of their assets unlike strategic default. The too-common use of strategic default unnecessarily passes on accountability of personal debt to others.

Chapter 10

The Reverse Mortgage Mistake

The television ads make them look so great; vacations, living a great lifestyle, happy couples smiling at their good fortune. The daytime business channels are inundated with commercials for reverse mortgages. It all started with actor Robert Wagner, continued with TV star Henry Winkler (say it ain't so, Fonzie) to the stoic former Tennessee Senator Fred Thompson. Using *CNBC* and *Fox Business* as their platform helps to legitimize the reverse mortgage as a financial planning tool. What could be better than people paid to stay in their own homes? But are reverse mortgages all they are cracked up to be?

A reverse mortgage is a tax-exempt home loan that allows a homeowner to take cash out of their house using their existing home equity, without taking on a monthly payment or having to sell. This loan program is available to homeowners aged sixty-two or older, who occupy a property as their principal residence.

A reverse mortgage works the opposite of a traditional mortgage, allowing a homeowner with accrued equity in their home to begin pulling cash out on a monthly or lump-sum basis. The money can be used for any expense such as home improvement, medical costs, or simply to pay off existing bills and property taxes. I found no restrictions on how the money is spent.

As long as the owner remains in the home, the loan never has to be repaid. The equity of their home is simply depleted. Once the owner moves out, the loan must be paid back plus interest and any other fees to the mortgage lender. The remaining equity, if any, would belong to the owner, but the debt can never exceed the value of the home. It sounds good, at least without researching the fine print.

Like "I before E, except after C" there are always exceptions.

The loan must be paid back in full if:

- One fails to pay property taxes or homeowners insurance.
- The property deteriorated without making the necessary repairs.
- The owner, or the last borrower, fails to live in the home for twelve consecutive months.

Any situation resulting in a loan default gives a lender the right to foreclose, purchase the property cheaply, and flip it for a profit.

Elderly homeowners are the most likely to pursue a reverse mortgage, but also fall into the group likely to be at risk. Perhaps as a final effort to salvage a bad situation they take the entire loan as a lump sum and spend that amount quickly, leaving nothing for future needs. They may also be targets of scam artists who offer "too-good-to-be-true" real estate or investment deals. Sadly, there are cases of family members cashing in on their inheritance early by encouraging a reverse mortgage.

A 2009 study on reverse mortgages from the Federal Reserve Board concluded closing costs on a reverse mortgage can run anywhere between $7,000 and $20,000. This compares to an average national closing cost of $3,741 on a standard mortgage. Part of the cost is associated with mortgage insurance, which the borrower pays both up-front and yearly. That charge, which does not vary between states or lenders, is the *greater* of $2,000 or two percent of the loan. The mortgage insurance will cover the borrower's line of credit or monthly payments if the lender goes under. The insurance will also pay the lender at the loan's maturity if the home value is not enough to repay the loan.

Anyone incurring the debt of a reverse mortgage, including aging parents, is okay as long as the debtor lives in the home. When it's time to move into an assisted living residence or a nursing home, the mortgage becomes due. Now there is the expense of paying off the balance added to the high cost of assisted living and/or nursing home. When the debt owner is forced to move, any non-borrowing family member, spouse, child, or grandchild living in the home has to move out.

If the owner or debtor passes away and the mortgaged home is their primary residence, then the heirs must pay off the loan balance. The entire principal, accrued interest, and service fees must be paid in full before heirs can legally take possession of the home. Sometimes that debt can exceed the market value of the home. If they can't pay, the lender has the right to foreclose and sell the property. Lower-wealth heirs are not likely able to pay the debt and those homes fall into foreclosure, leaving no inheritance.

The National Consumer Law Center issued a report on reverse mortgages called *Subprime Revisited*. They are worried the problems in the reverse mortgage industry are "eerily similar" to those that drove the subprime boom and led to its eventual housing bust. Reverse mortgages include a complex loan product, potentially vulnerable borrowers, and aggressive (at times deceptive) marketing. Elder abuse prevention advocate and California attorney Prescott Cole sees disaster coming down the road. Based on sales and life expectancy, he estimates that in ten years about 100,000 homes with reverse mortgages will be returned to lenders *each* year.

President Obama signed into law in 2011 a bill creating a Consumer Financial Protection Bureau. The law directs the agency to study the reverse mortgage industry and to decide if new laws are needed. Senator

Claire McCaskill, a Missouri Democrat and member of the Special Committee on Aging, would like new rules created banning misleading advertising and clear disclosure about the costs and terms. Another practice she's pushing for are restrictions on agents cross selling annuities and long-term care insurance with the money obtained with a reverse mortgage. These agents are double-dipping, making money on the front and back end. It should be no surprise the reverse mortgage industry opposes the new rule changes; after all, they don't want to kill the *golden goose*.

The bottom line: A reverse mortgage is just more debt and one of the most expensive forms of credit people acquire. State and federal laws continue to change as the housing market adjusts. Anyone considering a reverse mortgage should research and cover all bases and possibly seek legal advice before signing on the dotted line.

PART THREE

To Market, to Market, to Buy a Fat Pig

Making the decision to save for a better financial future
is easy. Knowing where and how to start could be
a bit trickier. The following chapters provide a
basic path on the road toward securing
a sound financial plan.

Chapter 11

Knowledge Is Power, Get Smart Now

When people finally get serious about building a stronger financial future, they will need to do some old-fashioned research. There is no magic formula for success (10,000 hours logged to become an expert). Some may spend a couple hours a week reading various periodicals, while others may be more apt to watch a half-hour market wrap-up show in the evening. The choice is in the hands of the person investing. If new to the fiscal game, I suggest starting slow. Find an investigative tool that will provide the information needed while also making this journey enjoyable.

Having read everything I could get my hands on over the years, I would like to give my two cents about some potential periodical choices. Here are some favorites:

Money Magazine: This is an easy way to begin reading about finance in general. *Money* provides good quality articles ranging from housing to finance and ratings on stocks and bond funds. The cost is reasonable.

Value Line: For those inclined to invest in individual stocks, *Value Line* does excellent research. The cost of the subscription can be expensive, so one needs to weigh the personal value gained versus the expense.

Investor's Business Daily: This publication caters to the stock trader mentality. Its founder, William O'Neil, championed the momentum-investing philosophy, which is buy high, sell higher. They offer a free two-week trial subscription.

Forbes Magazine: This consists of columnists' views and articles geared toward individual stocks.

Barron's: This weekly newspaper covers the scope of stocks, bonds, mutuel funds, ETFs (exchange-traded funds), etc. They offer first-rate articles and recommendations on buying and selling stocks. A one-year subscription is $52 with Saturday delivery. I think $1 a week is an excellent cost versus knowledge investment.

The Wall Street Journal: This is the granddaddy of them all, the oldest of all the financial newspapers and published six days a week. This paper covers everything business-wise and could substitute as a daily newspaper. It offers a three-month trial subscription for the price of one month and the paper offers home delivery.

Bigcharts.com and Stockcharts.com: For those more inclined to study charts on stocks, bonds, ETFs or mutuel funds, these two sites are excellent choices. Most of the information is free and the data provided is not too complex.

Stock Trader's Almanac: Since 1967, Yale Hirsch and now his son Jeffrey Hirsch have written the yearly *Stock Trader's Almanac*, of which I have been a subscriber for the last twenty-five years. The book is a cornucopia of historical data and price patterns, some dating back to 1833. This wealth of information should appeal to all types of investors and I recommend it. The yearly cost is $25 to $30.

Most of these periodicals are also available in digital editions. If you are not leaning toward a specific format preference, just compare costs. I would suggest readers try a couple and see which one fits their needs. One or two reference materials should be plenty. Trying to digest too much can push a new investor into the black hole of information overload. I can personally testify to this causing more harm than good for an individual's portfolio.

Today's choices for financial television shows are many. *CNBC*, *Fox Business*, and *Bloomberg* are three of the most widely watched. In the early 1970s, the only choices were PBS's *The Nightly Business Report* every weekday at 5:30 p.m. and *Wall $treet Week with Louis Rukeyser* every Friday night. Rukeyser (1933–2006) was famous for his pun-filled humor, and for trying to get investors to ignore the short-term gyrations and think long term. "Lou" took pride in effectively creating the first television show that focused on Wall Street.

Currently, financial business news provides programming from 4 a.m. to 8 p.m. Eastern Time. During the evening and early morning there are broadcasted talk shows, investigative reports, documentaries, infomercials and other programs. A rolling ticker provides real-time updates on share prices for the NYSE, NASDAQ and AMEX, as well as market indices, news summaries, and weather updates. With special programming from 8 p.m. to 11 p.m. added to the mix, I get the distinct impression each network is trying to create a captive audience. No other channels will be necessary. I imagine it's a fine line between trying to provide valuable unbiased information to their viewing audience, while programming for ratings and the almighty advertising dollars. Although most reporters may be altruistic and committed to their stories, the structure they work under is designed to keep viewers on the edge of their seats.

It seems today's financial programs want the public to live in fear and react to every little hiccup in the market. We must stay glued to their networks, waiting to receive sage advice from anchors and guests.

Wall Street and the financial press spew out so much analysis and so many opinions each week, it can make the average investor lose sight of the big picture and his/her own financial future.

Investors should understand there are only six factors determining the long-term value of one's investment portfolio.

1. How much money is saved.
2. How long investments compound.
3. Asset allocation: how assets are divided between stocks, bonds, cash, etc.
4. The total cost in annual expenses.
5. How much is paid out in taxes.
6. The annual return on assets.

These six aspects of financial planning will determine an individual's eventual net worth, whether investing $1,000 or one million. Of all the six factors, the only one nobody has control over is number six, "the annual return on assets." No one can predict with certainty future asset returns, including the talking heads on TV. After doing the proper research and achieving new financial confidence, readers now have the power to change the course of their financial future.

Chapter 12

Real Rate of Return versus Simple Rate

In Chapter 1 of this book, I quoted the historical 10% "average" return on stocks over the past one hundred or so years. Financial publications, the mutuel fund industry, and everyone else like to quote that number trying to convince investors on how to manage their assets. That magic number was derived from around 7% appreciation on stocks and roughly 3% on the dividends reinvested. In the first half of the 20th century, from 1900–1949, the dividend rate on stocks was higher and the appreciation rate was lower. Since 1950 stock appreciation has gone up as dividends decreased, falling as low as 1.2% in the early 2000s.

Following is a table of the average returns versus the real returns for the Dow Jones Industrials, trading at an all time low of 28.48 in August of 1896. The example excludes the reinvesting of any dividends and concentrates on the average versus real returns.

Periods	Number of Years	Avg. Rate of Return	Real Rate of Return	Percentage Difference
1896–1949	53.5	7.4%	3.7%	3.7%
1950–2013	62.5	8.5%	7.2%	1.3%
1896–2013	116	8.1%	5.6%	2.5%

The average return, also called the *simple* return, is calculated by adding up all the returns over a specific time span and dividing the total by the number of periods. This is not an accurate result. To calculate the *real* or the internal rate of return (IRR), a financial calculator or some financial spreadsheet package is necessary. By entering the value for the beginning period, called the *present value*, taking the value from the end period, called the *future value,* and entering the number of years, the IRR is calculated. This is the real invested percentage necessary year over year to get from point A, the past, to point B, the present.

Notice the difference for the entire period of 1896–2012 is 2.5% or 30% lower than the reported return of 8.1%. Over that 116-year period, the real return on the Dow Jones Averages was only 5.6%. What does a measly 2.5% difference make? It's a lot more than one might think.

Consider the hypothetical example of a one-time investment of $100 made in 1896 and letting it ride through three or four generations at the mythical rate of 8.1% without dividends. It would appear the fourth generation heirs would have accumulated $839,036. Doesn't that sound amazing? Unfortunately, that amount was calculated using the *average* and not the *actual rate* of return. In reality, the end balance is $55,593 or $783,443 less than the simple rate calculation. That's what an extra 2.5% does over 116 years and clearly shows the power of compounding over long periods.

Since most retirees' saving periods are between thirty and thirty-five years, let's calculate the differences between the two rates of return for a particular period. The Economic Recovery Act of 1981 opened the door for a matching IRA spousal contribution (up to $2,000). Let's calculate a thirty-one year savings period from 1982–2012 and use the real rates of return for the Dow Jones, S&P 500, and NASDAQ Composite.

The Dow's simple rate in the period was 10.2% and the real rate or the internal rate of return was only 7.7%, which is close to the 8.1% from the longer 1950–2012 period. After thirty-one years of saving $4,000 a year or $124,000, the real total tax-deferred amount would be $500,173. The friendly mutuel fund using the simple rate of 10.2% would estimate the portfolio worth about $832,608 or $332,435 more. The difference in the S&P 500 is $312,259 ($737,270 minus $425,011) and the NASDAQ had lower returns of $828,470 ($1,418,737 minus $590,267).

Following are the simple and actual rates for all three averages. Appendix A at the end of the book shows the calculations proofed out for the simple and real returns.

Date	Dow Real Rate of Return	S&P 500 Real Rate of Return	NASDAQ Real Rate of Return
1982	19.6%	14.8%	18.7%
1983	20.3%	17.3%	19.9%
1984	**-3.7%**	1.4%	**-11.2%**
1985	27.7%	26.3%	31.4%
1986	22.6%	14.6%	7.4%
1987	2.3%	2.0%	**-5.3%**
1988	11.8%	12.4%	15.4%
1989	27.0%	27.3%	19.3%
1990	**-4.3%**	**-6.6%**	**-17.8%**
1991	20.3%	26.3%	56.8%
1992	4.2%	4.5%	15.5%
1993	13.7%	7.1%	14.8%
1994	2.1%	**-1.5%**	**-3.2%**
1995	33.5%	34.1%	39.9%
1996	26.0%	20.3%	22.7%
1997	22.6%	31.0%	21.6%
1998	16.1%	26.7%	39.6%
1999	25.2%	19.5%	85.6%
2000	**-6.2%**	**-10.1%**	**-39.3%**
2001	**-7.1%**	**-13.0%**	**-21.1%**
2002	**-16.8%**	**-23.4%**	**-31.5%**
2003	25.3%	26.4%	50.0%
2004	3.1%	9.0%	8.6%
2005	**-0.6%**	3.0%	3.3%
2006	16.3%	13.6%	9.5%
2007	6.4%	3.5%	9.8%
2008	**-33.8%**	**-38.5%**	**-40.5%**
2009	18.8%	23.5%	43.9%
2010	11.0%	12.8%	16.9%
2011	5.5%	0.0%	**-1.8%**
2012	7.2%	13.3%	15.8%
Total Return	**316.1%**	**297.6%**	**394.7%**
# of Years	**31**	**31**	**31**
Simple Rate	**10.2%**	**9.6%**	**12.7%**
Real Rate	**7.7%**	**6.9%**	**8.5%**
Difference	**2.5%**	**2.7%**	**4.2%**

It is easy to see how this anomaly occurs. When buying ten shares of a $10 stock, without commissions, $100 is invested. Let's assume the stock doubled to $20 a share; the gain is now 100% with $200 in stock value. Next year the stock loses 50% of its current value dropping back to $10 a share. The account balance goes back to square one at $100 or a real return of zero.

The simple rate of return adds plus 100% in year one and negative 50% in year two for a total of plus 50%, or a 25% gain for the two-year period. If we reverse the years with the stock, decreasing 50% the first year and increasing 100% in the second year, the results are the same. In reality the stock value is still back to the original investment with only a mythical 25% gain. Welcome to creative accounting.

Following is a table on the Dow from the period 1955 to 1964. This period had seven up years and three down years, a typical ten-year period since the market was up 65% of the years since 1896. The table calculates the simple and real rate of $100 for that period.

Ten-Year Period	Yearly Returns	Ten-Year Average	Simple $100	Actual/Real $100
1955	20.8%	9.08%	$109	$121
1956	2.3%	9.08%	$119	$124
1957	-12.8%	9.08%	$130	$108
1958	33.9%	9.08%	$142	$144
1959	16.4%	9.08%	$154	$168
1960	-9.3%	9.08%	$168	$152
1961	18.7%	9.08%	$184	$181
1962	-10.8%	9.08%	$200	$161
1963	17.0%	9.08%	$219	$189
1964	14.6%	9.08%	$238	$216
Average	9.08%			8.00%

Calculating the simple return, $100 grows into $238 or a 9.08% average return. The total return during the period was only $216 or 8%. By flipping the returns upside down for the same ten-year period, it makes no difference in the final balance.

Ten-Year Period	Yearly Returns	Ten-Year Average	Simple $100	Actual/Real $100
1955	14.6%	9.08%	$109	$115
1956	17.0%	9.08%	$119	$134
1957	**-10.8%**	9.08%	$130	$120
1958	18.7%	9.08%	$142	$142
1959	**-9.3%**	9.08%	$154	$129
1960	16.4%	9.08%	$168	$150
1961	33.9%	9.08%	$184	$201
1962	**-12.8%**	9.08%	$200	$175
1963	2.3%	9.08%	$219	$179
1964	20.8%	9.08%	$238	$216
Average	**9.08%**			**8.00%**

The final chart uses an extended period of years with *no negative returns,* to test if simple returns still calculate higher than real returns. The time span of 1991 to 1999 is the only Dow nine-year period since 1896 without a loss. It came during Bill Clinton's eight-year reign as president.

Nine-Year Period	Yearly Returns	Ten-Year Average	Simple $100	Actual/Real $100
1991	20.3%	18.2%	$118	$120
1992	4.2%	18.2%	$140	$125
1993	13.7%	18.2%	$165	$143
1994	2.1%	18.2%	$195	$146
1995	33.5%	18.2%	$231	$194
1996	26.%	18.2%	$273	$245
1997	22.6%	18.2%	$322	$300
1998	16.1%	18.2%	$381	$349
1999	25.2%	18.2%	$450	$437
Average	**18.2%**			**17.80%**

Even in a roaring bull market, this chart proves the average returns will always be overstated. The longer an investment grows, and the more volatility in the markets, the bigger the difference becomes. By understanding this chapter, an investor will know to question those mythical returns quoted within the financial industry. Simple knowledge grows real returns.

Chapter 13

Drive Fast,
Build Wealth Slowly

The best way to accumulate wealth is to invest over long periods. In the previous chapter I talked about an initial $100 invested over four generations (116 years) turning into $55,593 using the real rate of return. In the first chapter, I discussed investing lottery money in an S&P 500 fund. Let's now cover some of the most common savings vehicles available for individuals who want to accomplish their long-term savings goals.

Traditional IRAs

An individual retirement account (IRA) allows directing pretax income, up to specific annual limits, toward investments that can grow tax-deferred. No capital gains or dividend income is taxed. Individual taxpayers are allowed to contribute 100% of compensation, up to a maximum dollar amount. Contributions to an IRA may be tax-deductible, depending on the taxpayer's income, tax-filing status and other factors. Investors can place IRA contributions into stocks, bonds, and other financial assets acceptable by the custodian. Assets, such as real estate, may be taxed differently with heavy restrictions from the Internal Revenue Service (IRS). When individuals begin to receive distributions from an IRA, the income is treated as ordinary income and subject to tax. Distributions are required when the owner reaches age 70½ according to the IRS formula.

Early withdrawals before age 59½ are taxed as ordinary income plus a 10% early withdrawal penalty. Currently, there are nine exceptions to the 10% penalty for IRA early withdrawal. The penalty does not apply to distributions that:

1. Occur because of the IRA owner's disability.
2. Occur because of the IRA owner's death.
3. Withdrawn as a series of "substantially equal periodic payments" made over the life expectancy of the IRA owner.
4. Are used to pay for unreimbursed medical expenses exceeding 7½% of adjusted gross income (AGI).
5. Are used to pay medical insurance premiums after the IRA owner has received unemployment compensation for more than twelve weeks.

6. Are used to pay the costs of a first-time home purchase (subject to a lifetime limit of $10,000).
7. Are used to pay for the qualified expenses of higher education for the IRA owner and/or eligible family members.
8. Are used to pay back taxes because of an Internal Revenue Service levy placed against the IRA.
9. Were nondeductible contributions. Calculating the taxable and nontaxable portion of the withdrawal is complicated. Form 8606 must be filed with the tax return to report both nondeductible traditional IRA contributions and withdrawals whenever they occur.

Roth IRA

Roth contributions are never deductible; however, their withdrawals will not be taxed. This assumes the Roth IRA has been open for at least five tax-years and the owner is older than age 59½. The Roth offers tax-*exempt* rather than simply tax-*deferred* savings. One word makes a big difference. Both types of IRAs allow investors to amass wealth without paying taxes, the difference being the traditional IRA is taxed on withdrawal. In a Roth IRA, as long as investors follow the rules, *no taxes will be paid on any gains.*

The Roth makes particular sense for people limited to making nondeductible contributions to a regular IRA. It allows participants to withdraw principal contributions tax-free, without penalty. First-time homebuyers can also pull out $10,000 in profits penalty-free and tax-free if the money has been in the Roth IRA for at least five tax years.

Here are the 2013 saving limits for both traditional and Roth IRAs:

Traditional & Roth IRA Contributions and Catch-Up Provisions:

Plan Name	Standard Limit	Catch-up Limit (Age 50 and older)
Traditional	$5,500	$6,500
Roth	$5,500	$6,500

Modified Adjusted Gross Income Limits for full deduction:

Traditional:	Single: $ 58,000,	Married Filing Jointly: $ 92,000
Roth:	Single: $112,000,	Married Filing Jointly: $178,000

Note: Earnings over the amounts listed are phased out for deductibility purposes. This does not apply to a traditional IRA for anyone not covered by a pension plan at his or her place of employment. They can still contribute the full amount, tax deductible, no matter how much they earn.

401(k)

The 401(k) is a *defined contribution plan* with annual limits up to $17,500 (2013). Contributions are tax-deferred and deducted from paychecks before taxes, similar to IRAs. Some employers may even match a portion of the employee's contribution. The employee eventually pays taxes on the money as he or she withdraws the funds during retirement. All gains are treated as ordinary income. All employers impose severe restrictions on withdrawals of pre-tax or Roth contributions while a person remains in service with their company and under the age of 59½. Withdrawals permitted before that age are subject to ordinary income tax plus a 10% penalty.

Many plans allow employees to take loans from their 401(k), paid back with after-tax funds, at predefined interest rates. The interest proceeds then become part of the 401(k) balance. The loan itself is not taxable income and not subject to the 10% penalty, as long as it's paid back in accordance with section 72(p) of the Internal Revenue Code. This section requires the loan term not to exceed five years, except for the purchase of a primary residence. A reasonable interest rate must be charged, and equal payments have to be made over the life of the loan.

Employer plans have the option for stricter loan terms. When an employee does not make payments in accordance with the plan or IRS regulations, the outstanding balance will be in default. A defaulted loan plus interest will become a taxable distribution in that year. All the tax penalties and implications of a withdrawal apply.

The interest portions of loan repayments are added contributions to the 401(k). Upon withdrawal, all funds are taxed equally, even though the interest portions were never tax-deferred. In essence, some contributions are double-taxed. Loans might be considered a plan benefit, but in my experience running a 401(k) plan at my workplace, loans led to hardship withdrawals ending in employees destroying their retirement accounts. Looking back, we should never have written a loan provision into our plan.

Starting in the 2006 tax year, employees could elect to designate their contributions as a Roth 401(k) deduction. Similar to the provisions of a Roth IRA, these contributions are considered after-tax. All earnings on these funds are not only tax-deferred but also tax-free on a qualified distribution. Unlike the Roth IRA, there is no upper income limit capping eligibility for Roth 401(k) contributions. Individuals who find themselves disqualified from a Roth IRA may contribute to their Roth 401(k). Individuals who qualify for both can contribute the maximum statutory amounts into both plans (including both catch-up contributions if applicable).

SEP IRA

Self-employed people do not get many breaks in the business world. They have to cover both halves of their Social Security taxes, employment taxes, and health insurance bills. They do get to pick from various self-employed retirement plans that offer far greater benefits, and the ability to tuck away more tax-deferred cash for retirement.

One of the most popular plans is the Simplified Employment Pension Plan (SEP IRAs) whose contribution limits ($51,000) are much higher than the traditional IRA. It is a great choice for self-employed individuals or family-owned businesses wanting to contribute up to 25% of their W-2 earnings, or 20% of net self-employment income, up to the SEP IRA contribution limit. One of the advantages is that they are easy to setup and have low administrative responsibilities.

The IRS rules do not allow loans with a SEP IRA. However, a SEP can be set up and converted to an individual 401(k) in the future. This allows the investor to change strategies and either receive a 401(k) loan or contribute more than the calculations of a SEP IRA will allow.

Like all qualified retirement plans, contributions and growth are tax-deferred until funds are withdrawn. Withdrawals taken before age 59½ face a 10% penalty plus tax on the monies. Withdrawals become mandatory at age 70½. Contribution levels can change every year to meet business conditions, and contributions can be made as late as the business's tax filing date for the year.

Conversions

When converting a traditional IRA to a Roth IRA, income tax is paid on the money and going forward all distributions are tax-free. If reconverting the Roth IRA back to a traditional IRA the process is called *recharacterization.* The deadline to recharacterize Roth IRAs back to traditional IRAs is October 15 if filing a federal income tax return or an extension. This strategy could be used if after the conversion the account decreased a significant amount.

Here are some key points to mull over before converting:

- Paying taxes on the money converted from a tax deductible IRA could bump individuals into a higher tax bracket.

- It is more favorable to use money outside one's IRA to pay the conversion taxes, such as drawing from a cash account.
- A portion of traditional IRA assets can be converted, giving investors tax diversification, avoiding a higher tax bracket.
- Any withdrawal within five years of a conversion faces taxes and penalties. Consider potential cash flow needs and future tax rates. If there is an expectation of a higher tax rate, converting may be an alternative. When a lower rate is anticipated, then the opposite holds true.

One last point: having tax-free money to draw from in the future helps attain a lower tax base, making less Social Security income taxable.

I believe long-term investors should take advantage of more than one of the savings vehicles covered in this chapter. Anyone having a 401(k) option at work, especially with any matching funds should enroll. I wholeheartedly recommend contributing the necessary amount to get the full match. Never turn down free money. Starting a traditional self-directed IRA or Roth IRA offers individuals more investing options than a workplace 401(k). This allows for greater diversification in a retirement portfolio.

Individual financial investments need due diligence and decisions based on personal goals and fiscal abilities. Staying informed about long-term investing rules will help in building wealth. As lives continually change, so should an investment strategy.

Chapter 14

The Rule of 72 and
Why You Should Care

The Rule of 72 is a simple formula used to estimate the time needed to double an investment. People are more likely to remember the rule rather than the exact mathematical formula. Assume an investor earning 8% on a mutuel fund account would like to estimate how long it takes to double the current balance. For this estimation to be accurate, the assumption is there will be neither withdrawals nor deposits into the account. An investment of $100 with an interest rate of 8% a year, the Rule of 72 calculates nine years needed for the investment to be worth $200. The basic calculation divides 72 (the rule) by 8 (the percentage on the investment) totaling 9 (the estimated number of years for a 100% increase). An exact mathematical calculation would total 9.006 years. The following chart shows the work longhand.

Year	Amount	Rate of Return	Interest Earned	Ending Balance
1	$100.00	8%	$8.00	$108.00
2	$108.00	8%	$8.64	$116.64
3	$116.64	8%	$9.33	$125.97
4	$125.97	8%	$10.08	$136.05
5	$136.05	8%	$10.88	$146.93
6	$146.93	8%	$11.75	$158.69
7	$158.69	8%	$12.69	$171.38
8	$171.38	8%	$13.71	$185.09
9	$185.09	8%	$14.81	$199.90

Assume an investor has a specific time frame of twelve years and wants to determine an estimate of the necessary annual percentage rate needed to double his money. The calculation is now 72 divided by 12 or 6%. Following is a $100 investment calculated at 6% a year for twelve years.

Year	Amount	Rate of Return	Interest Earned	Ending Balance
1	$100.00	6%	$6.00	$106.00
2	$106.00	6%	$6.36	$112.36
3	$112.36	6%	$6.74	$119.10
4	$119.10	6%	$7.15	$126.25
5	$126.25	6%	$7.57	$133.82
6	$133.82	6%	$8.03	$141.85
7	$141.85	6%	$8.51	$150.36
8	$150.36	6%	$9.02	$159.38
9	$159.38	6%	$9.56	$168.95
10	$168.95	6%	$10.14	$179.08
11	$179.08	6%	$10.75	$189.83
12	$189.83	6%	$11.39	$201.22

Notice how the interest earned the first year starts earning money on its own. As Ben Franklin said, "The money that money earns, earns money." This small cumulative growth makes compound interest extremely powerful—Einstein called it one of the most powerful forces in the universe.

The Rule of 72 is also useful for expenses like inflation or interest:

- If inflation rates go from 2% to 3%, amassed wealth will lose half its value in twenty-four rather than thirty-six years.
- If college tuition increases at 5% per year, which is faster than inflation, tuition costs will double in 72÷5 or about 14.4 years.
- If paying 15% interest on credit cards, the amount owed will double in only 72÷15, or 4.8 years!

To determine the time for money's buying power to halve, financiers divide the rule-quantity by the inflation rate. Therefore, at 3.5% inflation using the rule of 72, it should take 20.57 (72÷3.5) years for the value of a unit of currency to drop in halve.

To estimate the impact of extra fees on financial policies (mutual fund fees and expenses, load and expense charges on variable universal life insurance investment portfolios) divide 72 by the fee. For example, if a Universal Life Policy charges a 3% fee over and above the cost of the underlying investment fund, the total account value will be halved in twenty-four years (72÷3).

The Rule of 72 is also a valuable tool in calculating tax deferral going forward inside a rollover IRA, 401(k), or SEP plan where one stops contributing. If a retiree has $100,000 in one of the plans at 8% going forward, the investment doubles in nine years. Left untouched for eighteen years and the balance can swell to around $400,000.

Tax deferral has its detractors; they argue individuals are just pushing off their tax payment until the future when the money is finally drawn out. I disagree on three counts. First, the annual tax drag each year lowers the current account balance. Second, the government allows most investors to write off the amount contributed each year at the individual's highest tax bracket. Finally, investors have a better chance of being in a lower tax bracket at retirement. This allows them to control their own destiny by drawing out only the amount needed to supplement their retirement up to age 70½. IRS rules apply after this age.

In Appendix B, the first two tables show the results of saving $4,000 a year over thirty years in a taxable account and in a tax-deferred IRA where the amount contributed is fully deductible. I used 8% for the rate of return on both accounts and assumed the retiree was in the 25% tax bracket at retirement. The tax-deferred IRA totals $489,383 before any withdrawals. The account is worth $367,038 after 25% in taxes are deducted. The savings account after deducting taxes annually is worth $335,207, or $31,831 less. If one's tax bracket drops to 15% in retirement, then the difference is $80,769 in favor of the tax-deferred IRA.

The third table in Appendix B illustrates opening a separate Roth IRA and taking the $1,000 tax savings from the original IRA contribution and investing it at 8% for the same thirty-year period. That would add another $122,346 tax free to one's retirement. Regardless, one cannot discount the power of tax-deferred or tax-free savings.

Chapter 15

Calling a "Fowl" on Financial Black Swans

The phrase *black swan* was a common Latin expression in sixteenth-century London as a statement of impossibility. Black swan events, introduced in *Fooled by Randomness* (2001) and *The Black Swan* (2007) by Nassim Nicholas Taleb, also concerned financial events. A simple explanation of this metaphorical theory is a black swan event must meet certain criteria: the event was a surprise, deemed improbable, and caused massive consequences (negative or positive) and the effect rationalized through hindsight. Taleb regards almost all major scientific discoveries, historical events, and artistic accomplishments as black swans, undirected and unpredicted.

As far as the markets go, how many black swans were there? According to some financial analysts, we had three "rare birds": the October 1987 crash, the Internet bubble in 2000, and the financial crisis of 2008. Many analysts were blindsided, yet a few pundits called them correctly in advance.

Elaine Garzarelli, while working as a stock analyst at Lehman Brothers investment company, became well known for predicting Black Monday, the stock market crash of 1987. On that fated day, the S&P 500 dropped 22%. Garzarelli turned bearish on September 9. By October 12, when she appeared on Cable News Network's *Money Line* program, she predicted an imminent collapse in the stock market. She gave *USA Today* a similarly dire forecast the next day.

A little more than a decade later, Bill Fleckenstein, a professional money manager and market commentator, had been telling *CNBC* viewers for more than a year in advance that the Internet stocks were creating a huge market run-up, correctly calling the NASDAQ bubble of 2000. Those who did not listen lost over 90% of their money. I know people who were wiped out by the catastrophic drop in the stock market and their portfolios never recovered. In fact, the NASDAQ index peaked at 5,048 in March 2000; twelve years later it was still trading around 3,700, which is 27% below the high!

I don't believe significant financial events occurring in a relatively short time span can be considered under the black swan theory. Yes, they had extreme impacts and analysts created predictions after the fact; however, were they beyond the realm of normal expectations?

Using historical data tracking market gyrations, I think those movements were foreseeable to an extent. In the short-term markets move randomly, but taking a longer view, it is easier to see patterns. Those long-term patterns can be explained by what is called *regression to the mean.*

In statistics, regression toward the mean is the phenomenon that if a variable is extreme on its first measurement, it will be closer to the average on a second measurement. In finance, the term regression to the mean, or mean reversion, has a different meaning. Jeremy Siegel, a finance professor at the Wharton School of the University of Pennsylvania, uses it to describe a financial time sequence in which "returns can be unstable in the short run but very stable in the long run. Periods of lower returns are followed by compensating periods of higher returns and vice versa." The following table shows all the bull (up) and bear (down) markets since August 1896, when the Dow closed at its all time low of 28.48.

Bull and Bear Cycles Since 1896

Begin		End		Bull %	Length	Bear %	Length
Month	Dow	Month	Dow	Gain	Months	Loss	Months
Aug1896	28	Jun1901	57	104%	58	-46%	29
Nov1903	31	Jan1906	75	142%	26	-48%	22
Nov1907	39	Nov1909	74	90%	25	-28%	23
Sep1911	53	Sep1912	69	30%	12	-25%	22
Jul1914	52	Nov1916	110	112%	28	-40%	13
Dec1917	66	Nov1919	120	82%	23	-47%	22
Aug1921	64	Sep1929	381	**495%**	97	-48%	2
Nov1929	199	Apr1930	294	48%	5	**-86%**	27
Jul1932	41	Sep1932	80	95%	3	-38%	6
Feb1933	50	Feb1934	111	122%	12	-23%	6
Jul1934	86	Mar1937	194	126%	32	-49%	13
Mar1938	99	Nov1938	158	60%	8	-23%	5
Arp1939	121	Sep1939	156	**29%**	5	-40%	32
Arp1942	93	May1946	213	129%	50	-23%	12
May1947	163	Apr1956	521	220%	88	**-20%**	8
Oct1957	420	Dec1961	735	75%	41	-27%	10
Jun1962	536	Feb1966	995	86%	44	-25%	8
Oct1966	744	Dec1968	985	32%	26	-36%	18
May1970	631	Jan1973	1,052	67%	25	-45%	23
Dec1974	578	Sep1976	1,015	76%	22	-27%	18
Feb1978	742	Apr1981	1,024	38%	19	-24%	20
Aug 982	777	Aug 987	2,722	250%	53	-36%	8
Oct1987	1,739	Jul1990	3,000	73%	33	-21%	3
Oct1990	2,365	Jul1998	9,338	**295%**	95	**-20%**	1.5
Aug1998	7,539	Jan2000	11,723	55%	17	-30%	21
Sep 2001	8,236	Mar2002	10,635	**29%**	6	-31%	7
Oct2002	7,286	Oct2007	14,165	94%	61	-54%	17
Mar2009	6,547	Jul2013	15,503	126%	52		157
Bull	28		Avg. Gain	**114%**	Avg.Loss	**-36%**	
Bear	27			Tot Mon	966	Tot Mths	554
				Avg. Mths	35	Avg. Mths	21
				Avg. Yrs	2.88	Avg. Yrs	1.71

In Appendix C, there is a long-term chart of Dow Jones Industrial Averages going back to 1900. As discussed in Chapter 12 the real return on the Dow since 1896 was 5.6%.

Now let's expound on the bull and bears in the previous table. There have been twenty-eight bull markets since 1896 and twenty-seven bears. Any gain or loss less than 20% isn't considered a bull or bear market, but rather a correction or a reaction.

The average simple gain on the bull markets during those years was 114%, more than a double return. The two largest gains came in the 1920s (+495%) and the 1990s (+295%). What happened in the following decades, the 1930s and 2000s, was not pretty. The stock market Crash of 1929 brought on the Great Depression; and some called the late 2000s the Great Depression II. The smallest gains were 29% in 1939 and 2001.

The average loss during the bear markets was negative 36% with negative 20% the smallest loss. The largest loss occurred after the Crash of 1929 when the market dropped 86%. The simple definition of regression to the mean is periods of outperformance are followed by periods of underperformance. In addition, periods of severe outperformance (1920s and 1990s) are followed by periods of severe underperformance (see chart on next page). This is how markets regress to the mean. If real stock returns averaging 8% are followed by extended periods of 14% to 16%, then the future returns will underperform. The following losses in the 1930s were severe; the average investors returns were negative 9.7% from 1929 to 1942.

As night follows day, bear markets follow bull markets. The average bull market lasts about two years with the average bear lasting about a year. In the bigger cycles shown in the table below, the longer bull and bear cycles can last anywhere from nine to thirty-three years. In every long-term bull market, there are shorter-term bear markets, which turn out to be great buying opportunities. Jim Cramer, host of CNBC's *Mad Money,* and all the other mostly long hedge funds profited in the 1990s by buying every dip that occurred in the market. The long-term bear market of the 1930s was another story. During that period five rallies occurred, two were up over 100%, but all those gains were eventually erased. It wasn't until April 28, 1942, that a new long-term bull market emerged. The following table clearly shows that longer-term periods of outperformance are followed by similarly long periods of underperformance.

Dow Jones Industrial Averages
Longer-term Bull & Bear Cycles since 1896

Begin		End		Point	Total	Length	Real	
Date	DJIA	Date	DJIA	Gain/ Loss	% Gain	Yrs	Gain/ Loss	
Aug1896	28	Sept1929	381	24	1,260.7	33.1	8.21%	Bull
Sept1929	**381**	**Apr1942**	**93**	**-288**	**-75.6%**	**12.6**	**-10.60%**	**Bear**
Apr1942	93	June1962	995	902	971.0%	20.1	12.51%	Bull
June 1962	**995**	**Aug1982**	**777**	**-218**	**-21.9%**	**20.1**	**-1.22%**	**Bear**
Aug1982	777	Jan2000	11,723	10,946	1,408.8%	17.4	16.85%	Bull
Jan2000	**11,723**	**Mar2009**	**6,547**	**-5,176**	**-44.2%**	**9.1**	**-6.78%**	**Bear**
Mar2009	6,547	July2013	15,503	8,263	137%	4.4	21.52%	Bull

Knowledge is power, so in late 1999 had you known then what you know now, would you be throwing all your money into the stock market after the best seventeen-year run in history? I would hope not. Yet that is exactly what many investors did by piling into the small NASDAQ stocks, sending the average up over 85% in 1999. By October 2002, the index bottomed at 1,139 falling 3,909 points from the high of 5,048. A 77% decline wiped out the small investor's appetite for risk.

Following is a long-term chart of the NASDAQ composite going back to 1978 when the index traded at 105. At the peak in March 2000, the index outperformed both the Dow and S&P 500. This chart is called a log chart because the distance between 250 and 500 shows the same as 500 and 1,000 and so forth. All the doubles measure the same on the graph, making it a more accurate chart and visually easier to read.

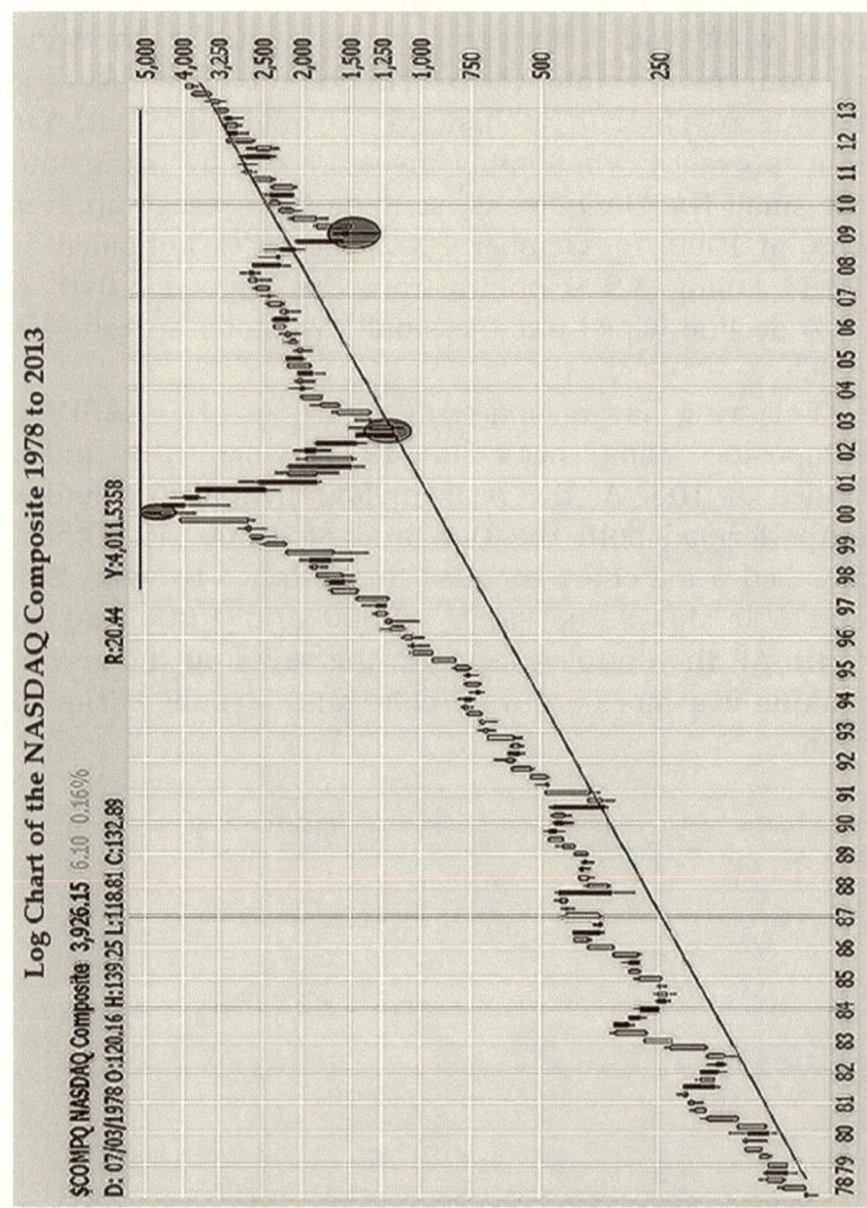

Chart courtesy of TD Ameritrade.

The pundits, who tend not to believe in longer bear markets, rarely talk about the NASDAQ. Instead, they like to use the S&P 500 because that index is a better fit to match their conclusions. However, the average investor buys stocks in the NASDAQ, which has not gotten back to the previous highs in the last thirteen years. If long periods of outperformance are followed by similar periods of underperformance, it may take another three to five years for the index to get back to even.

Behavioral psychologists use a term called *loss aversion.* In essence, it means that for many investors, the pain of losing money (even if it is just a paper loss) outweighs the pleasure of potential gains in the future. This causes them to sell everything they own and park their money in cash, sometimes at market bottom.

Many investors missed the move up from the bottom in 2003, with the market rising 94%. Those gains were erased in less than 1½ years as the Dow sold off to 6,547. When all the pundits were throwing in the towel, the market turned around so fast it left most investors and professionals behind. The Dow is currently up 137% from the March 2009 lows.

Investing in stocks for the long run has a *positive expectation,* that a gain is possible. The longer the time frame, the better chance of making money. Someone starting at age thirty-five and investing until age sixty-five (thirty years) will most likely make money. So far, all thirty-year rolling periods have shown positive returns since 1896. By using dollar cost averaging (buying monthly), investors can smooth out the long down periods. Unfortunately, in shorter time spans individuals can lose money, sometimes more than could be imagined. Currently, many small investors are still waiting to revisit better times. Those times should come thanks to regression to the mean.

Chapter 16

Trading Stocks Is a Mugs Game

According to the Urban Dictionary a *mugs game* is defined as "Any game someone is more likely to lose than win, no matter how sweet the odds or how much it *looks* like they'll win." Example:

> "Hey man, I'm gonna go play poker with Steve. You in?"
>
> "Hell no, that's a mug's game. Steve's a professional magician, are you stupid? He'll rob you blind."
>
> "Alright man, your loss. I like my chances."

Stock newsletters are the persuasive marketing tool that makes trading individual stocks seem like an easy game. Following is an example of statements made in a few of those publications.

100% Profit in Your Pocket Every 22 Days or Less with This Never-Ending Winning Streak 17 TRADES WE WISH YOU CLOSED OUT IN 2012

In 2012, 17 of our recommendations reached price highs resulting in gains of 100% or more. Here is the complete list of 17 recommendations we made in 2012 or previous years with their profits if they were sold in 2012 at their price highs:

Symbol	Profit
EXPE	145.79%
NTSP	135.45%
SMBL	133.63%
EXPE (option)	171.43%
BMO	124.39%
CBM	178.79%
GMCR (option)	155.81%
EGHT	103.48%
GILD	109.45%
QIHU (option)	147.22%
INWK	112.11%
KH	109.47%
RSH (short)	119.48%
ALXN	218.77%
RIC	174.39%
PRTS (short)	101.37%
CRUS	215.90%
AVERAGE PROFIT:	**144.53%**

The typical stock or option newsletter is distributed via bulk mail or email. They always post their biggest winners and make the grand assumption that everyone sold at the peak of the stock's highest price. That's impossible, since no one can know the top of any stock until after it peaks. Notice in the advertisement, only seventeen winners are listed. This would be an amazing result if the number of total buy recommendations for the year included only thirty or so stocks. The total number of stock or option plays and the inclusive return for all the information was not readily available. Here is what I did find:

"There is no magic formula to getting rich in the stock market. Like all forms of investment, success in selecting stocks with the best prospects for price appreciation can only be achieved through proper and rigorous research and analysis of publicly available company and industry filings and news releases. The opinions in this advertisement are just that, opinions of the author. **Warning:** *Stock trading involves high risks and you can lose a lot of money—you may even lose all the money you invested. So please, do not invest with money you cannot afford to lose. Past results are not necessarily indicative of Future results."*

After reading the sales pitch with its full disclosure and warnings, the individual investor must now make a decision. Is it practical to pay $10 to $20 a week or $520 to $1,040 a year, plus trading costs, for potential information that could result in losing one's entire investment? I might just try playing cards with Steve the magician.

As I discussed in Chapter 11, "Knowledge is Power," there is plenty of free financial advice televised daily. When it comes to individual stock buys there is one adviser who recommends splitting purchases and buy stocks as they decrease in price. For example, if buying 200 shares of XYZ is the goal, one would buy 50 or 100 at first, and buy more shares as the stock goes lower, averaging down, not up. I have trouble making any sense of a strategy where I hope my stock goes lower so I can continue to buy it cheaper later. Why not wait to buy the whole position? In addition, if company XYZ increases from my initial purchase price I might never get to buy the full amount of shares. Most professional traders consider averaging down a bad bet.

These strategies worked well the '90s. Then every dip in the market was a true buying opportunity as the market then soared higher. During the 2000–2009 period, the same tactics did not work as well. There is an old saying, "everybody's a genius in a bull market"; not so much in a bear market.

The chance of beating the averages after factoring in trading costs is a real long shot. In the old days, it cost up to $100 commission per transaction to buy or sell stocks. Individual investors did not trade a lot at those prices. Today the cost is around $10 each way. If an investor opens a new brokerage account or transfers in assets, they may even get some free trades. The catch now is that the cheaper it is to buy and sell, the more the average investor will trade. The more stocks traded, even at a $20 round-trip fee, the higher the transaction costs run. Those commissions eat into the total returns.

Exchange-traded funds (ETFs) are now replacing mutual funds for the average investor. No more waiting until the stock market closes (4 p.m. EST) to get out of a fund; an ETF can be sold at anytime, for as low as $6.99. In my experience, lower trading costs hurt average investors, not help them. It's easy to trade up to 100 stocks a year in a trading account (eight a month, two a week). At $20 a pop, that costs $2,000 a year in trading expenses. If an investor opened an account with a starting balance of $10,000 and earned 15% trading, his final balance would be $9,500 ($11,500 minus $2,000) after trading costs. Even when doubling the market average returns of 8% the result is a 5% loss. Yikes!

I recently read an article featuring the top ten stocks of the last ten years. The article stated how well one would have done if they had owned these ten compared to the averages. Really? There are more than 6,400 stocks listed on the three major exchanges (NYSE, NASDAQ, and Amex). The chance ten years ago of someone buying just one of those top ten stocks is "slim to none and slim left town." Investors are more likely to buy them near or at their top when everybody else is hyping them, rather than at the bottom when nobody has heard of them. As I noted in Chapter 15, the whole idea about regression to the mean explains why it's unlikely for those returns to go on much longer.

Peter Lynch, the heralded Fidelity Magellan Mutuel Fund manager, recommends that people buy what they know. Today, for example, that could be Costco if someone shops there, and Apple or Ross stores if one buys and likes their products. That's what Peter Lynch did; he bought the Costco, Apple, and Ross stores of his day and did very well. Fortunately for him, that period coincided with the biggest bull market of the 20th century: 1982 to 1999.

In the past, individual stock analysis was hard to find and required a lot of legwork. Now it's readily available to everybody over the Internet. This means today most of the information is already built into stock prices, evening out the playing field and taking away the advantage for investors that went the extra mile in research.

Two last items clarifying the difficulty of trading individual stocks. In a retirement account (IRA, 401(k)) stock losses cannot be written off. In a nonretirement account the IRS lets taxpayers write off up to $3,000 per year, after matching winners against losers. The rest of the loss must be carried forward to future years. Any big gain, however, is taxed in total in the year it was realized. I had a friend who lost $30,000 on one of his stock buys and it took him ten years to write off that total loss. After being mugged, he never again traded individual stocks.

Another caveat: This chapter deals with frequently trading stocks that pay little or no dividends (sometimes called high fliers). Buying and holding high quality dividend stocks for the long-term keeps costs down and provides a stream of income. Some companies have DRIP plans (dividend reinvestment program) which reinvest those dividends in more shares of stock. When selling the shares after death any heirs will get a stepped-up basis on the inherited shares (the day *they* took ownership) and no prior years of appreciation are taxed. Investors should always consult an accountant for varying tax strategies.

Chapter 17

Expenses Do Matter

I never paid much attention to mutual fund expenses until recently. I talked about the cost of buying and selling individual stocks in the last chapter and how lower brokerage commissions might have hurt the average investor by leading to more frequent trading. Exchange-traded funds (ETFs) are becoming more popular with some fund families and can be traded commission-free. Let's now concentrate on the effects of expense fees on long-term investments.

Many investors use stock mutual funds in their IRAs or 401(k). High fund fees result in a drag on performance, especially long-term. Every fund charges an expense ratio or management fee, ranging anywhere from .08% to 2.5%. Some funds add on a onetime front-end load between 4% to 5%. Others opt for a back-end load of equal amounts. If a fund is not held for more than ninety days, some companies charge a 1% distribution fee. However, the redemption or distribution fee will not matter to investors who plan to hold a fund for the long-term.

One fee that investors should try to avoid is the front-end load on funds sold by financial planners or advisers. Investor funds, bought by the individual investor, do not carry a load fee. I cannot think of any reason to pay a front-end or back-end load fee. Many studies have yet to prove that load funds outperform no-load funds. Why pay $450 on a $10,000 fund purchase if the fund's performance cannot overcome the load fee?

The next distinction investors may choose to make is between actively managed funds and passive or index funds. Fund managers of actively managed funds select specific stocks in an attempt to outperform the benchmark of an index, like the S&P 500. Actively managed funds charge more in fees and trading costs hoping to make up the difference with better returns over the index they are tracking. There is a potential to outperform the market; unfortunately, the average 1% extra fee often results in a lower real return than the index fund. Evidence that actively managed funds can *consistently* outperform their relevant indices is difficult to find. It is even more challenging for individual investors to identify which actively managed fund will outperform the index in a given year.

According to Vanguard, for the ten years leading up to 2007, most actively managed U.S. stock funds underperformed the index they were seeking to outperform. They found 84% of actively managed U.S. large blend funds underperformed their index and 68% of actively managed U.S. small value funds did the same. The case is even worse for bond funds. Almost 95% of actively managed bond funds underperformed their indexes for ten years.

Index mutual funds and exchange-traded funds offer low-cost alternatives when compared to actively managed funds. With large index funds, some may *sample*, meaning they invest in some, but not all, of the holdings making up the underlying index. Some funds will do this more effectively than others. Not all index funds charge the same, and fees can vary. Before investing in any index product, consider not only its past performance but also how closely it tracks the index it's replicating.

The Vanguard Group's web site has a tool that will compare past fees on their funds or other family funds based on the past performance. Investors also can use the site to estimate future stock market returns on funds with different expense fees. In the following table, I ran three scenarios using expense fees for a minimal cost index fund (.20%), a low-cost actively managed fund (1.2%), and the average domestic stock fund (2.2%). The initial one-time investment used was $10,000 and the rate of return was 8% going forward for periods of ten, twenty, and thirty years.

$10,000 Invested Once	Minimal Cost Index fund	Low-Cost Active Managed Fund	Average cost Domestic Fund
Expense Ratio (fee)	0.20%	1.20%	2.20%
Investment	$10,000	$10,000	$10,000
Hypothetical Return	8%	8%	8%
Time Horizon	10 Years	10 Years	10 Years
Total Return Before Costs	$21,589	$21,589	$21,589
Total Fee Cost	$397	$2,283	$4,016
Fee % of Total Return	1.84%	10.57%	18.60%
Total Return After Costs	**$21,192**	**$19,306**	**$17,573**
Time Horizon	20 Years	20 Years	20 Years
Total Return Before Costs	$46,610	$46,610	$46,610
Total Fee Cost	$1,697	$9,334	$15,727
Fee % of Total Return	3.64%	20.03%	33.74%
Total Return After Costs	**$44,913**	**$37,276**	**$30,883**
Time Horizon	30 Years	30 Years	30 Years
Total Return Before Costs	$100,626	$100,626	$100,626
Total Fee Cost	$5,442	$28,658	$46,355
Fee % of Total Return	5.41%	28.48%	46.07%
Total Return After Costs	**$95,184**	**$71,968**	**$54,271**

The **bolded** totals show the total return after expenses for the three time frames. The longer the period, the more pronounced the differences. After thirty years almost half (46%) of the funds return is eaten up in expenses with a fund fee of 2.2% (the average domestic fund). An extra $40,913 can be accumulated using a low-cost index fund instead of the average domestic fund.

What if an individual nearing retirement had $100,000 invested in different funds with higher expense ratios? Look below to see the same scenario based on $100,000 going forward for the same three periods.

$100,000 Invested Once	Minimal Cost Index fund	Low-Cost Active Managed Fund	Average cost Domestic Fund
Expense Ratio (fee)	0.20%	1.20%	2.20%
Investment	$100,000	$100,000	$100,000
Hypothetical Return	8%	8%	8%
Time Horizon	10 Years	10 Years	10 Years
Total Return Before Costs	$215,893	$215,893	$215,893
Total Fee Cost	$4,279	$24,552	$43,060
Fee % of Total Return	1.98%	11.37%	19.95%
Total Return After Costs	**$211,614**	**$191,341**	**$172,833**
Time Horizon	20 Years	20 Years	20 Years
Total Return Before Costs	$466,095	$466,095	$466,095
Total Fee Cost	$18,294	$99,985	$167,384
Fee % of Total Return	3.92%	21.45%	35.91%
Total Return After Costs	**$447,801**	**$366,110**	**$298,711**
Time Horizon	30 Years	30 Years	30 Years
Total Return Before Costs	$1,006,266	$1,006,266	$1,006,266
Total Fee Cost	$58,658	$305,745	$489,994
Fee % of Total Return	5.83%	30.38%	48.69%
Total Return After Costs	**$947,608**	**$700,521**	**$516,272**

Over a ten-year period, the investor saved $38,781 in the lowest fee fund (.20%) versus the highest (2.2%),

$149,090 for twenty years, and $431,336 over thirty years. That's some serious cash!

According to "The Hidden Cost of Doing Business" in the March 4, 2013 issue of *Barron's*, trading costs can more than double one's expenses. The article studied 1,800 funds and found the average expense ratio was 1.19%, but the average cost to buy and sell was an extra 1.44%. Small cap growth funds had the most expenses averaging 3.17%. Because an index fund does fewer buying and selling, by replicating the index, their trading costs are much less.

If an investor believes he or she can pick one of the few funds outperforming the indices every year, paying up for performance could put them ahead. However, one must also consider the odds of selecting a fund that does worse than the averages. There is about a 75% chance of this happening. That being the case, not only are investors paying higher fees, but are stuck with an underperforming fund, a double whammy.

There is nothing wrong with getting the market's average return, especially when not having to pay a lot in fees or trading costs to do it. Many investors are more comfortable with and prefer using a financial advisor or planner. The additional fees incurred may be worth the peace of mind if the end result gets one closer to their financial goal.

Note: Vanguard is not the only fund family with low expenses, but they were the first and have a wide selection. ETFs with low expenses can be bought from many fund families or in a brokerage account. Vanguard does not charge a commission to buy and sell their ETFs.

Chapter 18

Where to Invest Your
Hard-Earned Money?

So if trading individual stocks is a mugs game, markets eventually regress to the mean, and expenses do matter, where does the individual investor go from here? What are and where do our best alternatives lie in investing for the future? Staying with the theory it's tough to beat the index funds by picking individual stocks or actively managed mutuel funds, let's look at individual returns from various stock market indices.

The table on the next page shows percentage gains since 1980 for eight different indices. Included are the Dow, NASDAQ, S&P 500, Mid Cap, Russell 1000, Russell Small Cap Value, the EAFE (Europe, Australia, Far East Asia), and Barclays U.S. Aggregate Bond

Index. Choosing from these options would leave an investor with a well-balanced portfolio. The percentage going into each category is a personal choice depending on one's comfort level for risk.

Year	Dow	S&P	NASDAQ	Mid Cap	Rus1K	RusValue	Eafe	Bonds
1980	14.9%	25.3%	**33.9%**		25.6%	25.4%	22.6%	2.7%
1981	-9.2%	-9.7%	-3.2%		-9.7%	14.9%	-2.3%	6.3%
1982	19.6%	14.8%	18.7%		13.7%	28.5%	-1.9%	32.7%
1983	20.3%	17.3%	19.9%		17.0%	38.6%	23.7%	8.2%
1984	-3.7%	1.4%	-11.2%		-0.1%	2.3%	7.4%	15.2%
1985	27.7%	26.3%	31.4%		26.7%	31.0%	56.1%	22.1%
1986	22.6%	14.6%	7.4%		13.6%	7.4%	69.5%	15.3%
1987	2.3%	2.0%	-5.3%		0.2%	-7.1%	24.6%	2.8%
1988	11.8%	12.4%	15.4%		13.1%	29.5%	28.3%	7.9%
1989	27.0%	27.3%	19.3%		25.9%	12.4%	10.5%	14.5%
1990	-4.3%	-6.6%	-17.8%		-7.5%	-21.8%	-23.5%	9.0%
1991	20.3%	26.3%	56.8%		28.8%	41.7%	12.1%	16.0%
1992	4.2%	4.5%	15.5%		5.9%	29.1%	-12.2%	7.4%
1993	13.7%	7.1%	14.8%		7.3%	23.8%	32.6%	9.8%
1994	2.1%	-1.5%	-3.2%		-2.4%	-1.5%	7.8%	-2.9%
1995	33.5%	34.1%	39.9%	34.5%	34.4%	25.8%	11.2%	18.5%
1996	26.0%	20.3%	22.7%	19.0%	19.7%	21.4%	6.1%	3.6%
1997	22.6%	31.0%	21.6%	29.0%	30.5%	31.8%	1.8%	9.9%
1998	16.1%	26.7%	39.6%	10.1%	25.1%	-6.5%	20.0%	8.7%
1999	25.2%	19.5%	85.6%	18.2%	19.5%	-1.5%	27.0%	-0.8%
2000	-6.2%	-10.1%	-39.3%	8.3%	-8.8%	22.8%	-14.2%	11.6%
2001	-7.1%	-13.0%	-21.1%	-5.6%	-13.6%	14.0%	-21.4%	8.4%
2002	-16.8%	-23.4%	-31.5%	-16.2%	-22.9%	-11.4%	-15.9%	10.3%
2003	25.3%	26.4%	50.0%	40.1%	27.5%	46.0%	38.6%	4.1%
2004	3.1%	9.0%	8.6%	20.2%	9.5%	22.3%	20.3%	4.3%
2005	-0.6%	3.0%	1.4%	12.7%	4.4%	4.7%	13.5%	2.4%
2006	16.3%	13.6%	9.5%	15.3%	13.3%	23.5%	26.3%	4.3%
2007	6.4%	3.5%	9.8%	5.6%	3.9%	-9.8%	11.2%	7.0%
2008	-33.8%	-38.5%	-40.5%	-41.5%	-39.0%	-28.9%	-43.4%	5.2%
2009	18.8%	23.5%	43.9%	40.5%	25.5%	20.6%	31.8%	5.9%

Year	Dow	S&P	NASDAQ	Mid Cap	Rus1K	RusValue	Eafe	Bonds
2010	11.0%	12.8%	16.9%	**25.5%**	13.9%	24.5%	7.8%	6.5%
2011	5.5%	**-0.3%**	**-1.8%**	**-1.6%**	**-0.5%**	**-5.5%**	**-12.1%**	**7.8%**
2012	7.2%	13.3%	15.8%	**17.3%**	16.8%	14.4%	**17.3%**	4.2%
Real Ret	**8.7%**	**8.1%**	**9.5%**	**10.8%**	**8.2%**	**12.5%**	**9.2%**	**8.6%**
Up Yrs	25	25	23	14	24	24	24	31
Down Yrs	8	8	10	4	9	9	9	2
Leader	1	1	7	2	0	8	9	6
Laggard	2	2	5	0	1	5	10	10

The averages do not consider dividends
reinvested or fund expenses.

At first glance, the table may seem confusing, but it contains a wealth of valuable information. The grayscale bolded positive cells are the best return of the eight indices for that particular year. All negative figures are bolded but not grayscale. The totals at the bottom reflect the real return, not including dividends, and the number of up years versus down years. I also added the number of times the particular indices led or lagged the category. Here is a summary of the eight-charted indices.

Dow Jones Industrial Averages

The Dow is the most well known and quoted index by the media, consisting of only thirty industrial stocks. In the past, investors could not buy the Dow Jones as an index; they had to buy all thirty stocks. Available today are funds, or ETFs, that attempt to track it. Tracking is seeking to mirror a benchmark of a specific market. In the last thirty-three-years, the Dow has risen twenty-five times and fallen eight. During that period, it captured the best return only one time and the worst returns twice. Its real return was 8.7% besting only the S&P 500, Russell 1000, and bonds.

S&P 500

The S&P is the most common index tracked, containing five hundred stocks. Investors can get a Vanguard S&P index fund with a .08% expense fee, one of the lowest around. The index was up twenty-five times and down eight, but only led in one year. Some comfort is the S&P only lagged twice, unfortunately over the charted period it had the lowest total performance of the eight, gaining only 8.1%. A low expense ratio is the one upside for accepting smaller returns.

NASDAQ

The NASDAQ contains those high-flying technology stocks individual investors and hedge funds like to buy. This explains why there are several big gains and losses, showing how volatile it can be. NASDAQ led the averages seven times, lagged five, capturing the leading position ten times in the down years. Investors took a lot of risk for a 9.5% reward over that period. Strap on your seat belts when riding the NASDAQ bull. I will cover this in detail in Chapter 21.

Mid Cap

The Mid Cap is a new index falling between the Russell Value and the S&P 500 larger stocks. It rose fourteen out of eighteen years with a 10.8% real return, and has been the leader twice but never the laggard. It did have the lowest return of the domestic (U.S.) indices in 2008 at negative 41.5%.

Russell 1000

The Russell 1000 contains the largest cap stocks of the smallest index. It was never the yearly leader but only lagged once, tying the S&P 500 in 1981 at negative 9.7%. The 1000 also ties the Russell Value and the EAFE with twenty-four up years and nine down years. The 8.2% return is the second lowest average return since 1980.

Russell Small Cap Value

This index contains the smallest stocks of any major index and it's a value index. The Russell Value has been the best performer with a real return of 12.5%, beating all but the Mid Cap stocks by 3% to 4%. The Russell also had the best return eight times, and lagged five times, but with smaller down years than the average. This is the clear winner over the thirty-three-year period.

EAFE (Europe, Australia, and Far East Asia)

Overseas investors look at this index first. The EAFE includes a selection of stocks from twenty-two developed markets, excluding those from the U.S. and Canada. This index led nine times but lagged ten, producing a real return of 9.2%. The fact it was the lowest performer of the eight in 2008, down 43.4%, proves that it did not provide the diversification most expected. One can also target specific countries or small emerging markets when investing overseas. This can increase returns but also increase the risk.

Barclays Aggregate U. S. Bond Index

This is a broad base index, maintained by Barclays Capital, and used to represent investment-grade bonds traded in the United States. Many index funds and exchange-traded funds try to mirror (before fees and expenses) the performance of the Barclays Capital Aggregate Bond Index. Bond funds carry a lot less risk than the seven previously noted investments. They had only two down years, a negative 2.9% in 1994, and negative .8% in 1999. The index led in six years beating four other indices, but lagged in ten. Minimal risk and consistent returns, a total average of 8.6% over the thirty-three year period, is an excellent record of accomplishment.

These eight indices are the best known and most widely held, except for the Russell Small Cap Value. I wanted to compare that index because it has been the best performer, not only since 1980, but also since 1926. The S&P and Mid Caps have their own growth and value indices; however, none has matched the Russell's long-term performance.

Why do small value stocks offer superior returns over time? First, small cap stocks are never over-owned by institutions. Since they are small market cap stocks, big mutuel funds and hedge funds cannot buy or sell these stocks without significantly driving the prices up or down. Second, they are not widely covered by analysts whose recommendations to buy and sell can affect stock prices, creating much volatility. Finally, some value stocks can be oversold in price (hence the name value) and that gives them a greater chance to increase in value to the upside. It is best to own small caps in a fund or index rather than individually. This avoids the potential of losing one's entire investment if the firm goes bankrupt and the shares stop trading.

On the next page is a worksheet showing the real return (no expenses or dividends reinvested) of a one-time investment of $100 over the thirty-three-year period for all indices. Note the Mid Cap's final total of $633 is compounded over its shortened eighteen-year existence.

Small cap value trounced all other indices turning $100 into $4,809 over the trial period, proving what an extra 3% to 4% can do over the long-term. The Mid Cap's return of 10.8% over the shorter period is the closest to the Russell Value. Back tested over the thirty-three-year span it would have returned $2,950 for the original $100. That makes sense since the Mid Cap is the next smallest stock index tested.

Year	Dow	S&P	NASDAQ	Mid Cap	Rus1K	RusValue	Eafe	Bonds
Start	**$100**	**$100**	**$100**		**$100**	**$100**	**$100**	**$100**
1980	$115	$125	$134		$126	$125	$123	$103
1981	$104	$113	$130		$113	$144	$120	$109
1982	$125	$130	$154		$129	$185	$118	$145
1983	$150	$152	$184		$151	$257	$145	$157
1984	$145	$154	$164		$151	$262	$156	$180
1985	$185	$195	$215		$191	$344	$244	$220
1986	$226	$224	$231		$217	$369	$413	$254
1987	$232	$228	$219		$217	$343	$515	$261
1988	$259	$256	$252		$246	$444	$661	$282
1989	$329	$326	$301		$310	$499	$730	$322
1990	$315	$305	$247		$286	$391	$559	$351
1991	$378	$385	$388		$369	$553	$627	$408
1992	$394	$402	$448		$391	$715	$551	$438
1993	$448	$431	$514		$419	$885	$730	$480
1994	$458	$424	$497	$100	$409	$871	$787	$466
1995	$611	$569	$696	$134	$550	$1,095	$875	$552
1996	$770	$685	$854	$160	$658	$1,329	$928	$573
1997	$944	$897	$1,039	$206	$859	$1,752	$944	$629
1998	$1,096	$1,136	$1,451	$227	$1,074	$1,639	$1,133	$684
1999	$1,373	$1,358	$2,693	$269	$1,284	$1,614	$1,439	$679
2000	$1,287	$1,221	$1,635	$291	$1,171	$1,983	$1,235	$758
2001	$1,196	$1,062	$1,291	$275	$1,011	$2,261	$970	$821
2002	$995	$814	$884	$230	$780	$2,003	$816	$906
2003	$1,247	$1,028	$1,326	$322	$994	$2,924	$1,130	$943
2004	$1,285	$1,121	$1,439	$387	$1,089	$3,575	$1,359	$984
2005	$1,278	$1,155	$1,459	$436	$1,137	$3,743	$1,543	$1,008
2006	$1,486	$1,312	$1,598	$503	$1,288	$4,622	$1,950	$1,051
2007	$1,581	$1,357	$1,755	$531	$1,338	$4,170	$2,167	$1,125
2008	$1,047	$835	$1,043	$311	$816	$2,964	$1,227	$1,184
2009	$1,243	$1,031	$1,501	$437	$1,024	$3,574	$1,617	$1,254
2010	$1,380	$1,163	$1,755	$548	$1,167	$4,450	$1,742	$1,336
2011	$1,456	$1,160	$1,724	$540	$1,161	$4,205	$1,531	$1,440
2012	$1,561	$1,314	$1,996	**$633**	$1,356	**$4,809**	$1,796	$1,501
Real Return	**8.7%**	**8.1%**	**9.5%**	**10.8%**	**8.2%**	**12.5%**	**9.2%**	**8.6%**

The bottom line: Investors should not put everything in small caps, but they should be a part of the portfolio to boost performance. I believe the last thirty-three-year test period had been good for bonds (8.6%), as interest rates fell from highs of 14% in the early 1980s down to 1%. When interest rates fall, bond prices rise; it is the opposite of what one would think. Since interest rates cannot go much lower, in the next thirty-three-year period bonds will likely underperform stocks. However, for some safety and income they should still be a piece of a prudent portfolio.

Note: Appendix D shows a more detailed explanation of how the return was derived for the Russell Small Cap Value Index.

PART FOUR

The Gold at the End of the Rainbow

Reaching a financial goal is rarely a straight shot
from point A to point B. It can often resemble
a ride on the Wild Mouse, requiring a
change in course. Once achieved,
those goals still need individual
monitoring and review. Keep
an eye on that hard-
earned prize.

Chapter 19

What's Your Net Worth Really Worth?

Calculating a net worth statement is a simple process everyone should be able to do. Using Quicken software for personal finance, net worth can be retrieved at the touch of a button. The reason I love Quicken, and have used it for many years, I'm able to balance my checkbook in under two minutes. It also ties into their Turbo Tax product for tax preparation. Under $100 for both programs (check for sales), anyone can have their finances and taxes done for less than the cost of an accountant or financial planner.

If *easy as possible* is your motto, a simple spreadsheet is all that is necessary to calculate net worth. On the next page is an example of an uncomplicated net worth spreadsheet, using some test numbers, which anyone can put together. Added to the worksheet is a cash flow section tracking monthly inflows and outflows. This establishes a surplus or deficit balance. This may come in handy, especially in retirement.

Net Worth Spreadsheet

Assets			Liabilities		
Cash/Cash Equivalents			Mortgages		
Checking Account	$1,500	0.5%	Home	$175,000	87.1%
Money Market\Cd's	$5,000	1.5%	Vacation Property		0.0%
Bank Account	$2,000	0.6%	Other		0.0%
Total Cash	**$8,500**	**2.6%**	**Total Mortgages**	$175,000	**87.1%**
Personal Property			Loans		
House	$250,000	75.2%	Auto	$20,000	10.0%
Cars	$25,000	7.5%	Installment		0.0%
Furnishing	$10,000	3.0%	Home Improvement	$5,000	2.5%
Total Use Assets	**$285,000**	**85.7%**	**Total Loans**	$25,000	**12.4%**
Liquid Investments			Unpaid Bills		
Stocks	$2,000	0.6%	Credit Cards	$1,000	
Bonds	$2,000	0.6%	Personal Loans		
Total Stock/Bond	**$4,000**	**1.2%**	**Total Unpaid Bills**	$1,000	**0.5%**
Nonliquid Investments					
Insurance-Cash Value	$5,000	1.5%			
Pension Plans		0.0%			

Assets			Liabilities		
Ira/401K's	$30,000	9.0%			
Total Nonliquid	**$35,000**	**10.5%**			
Total Assets	**$332,500**	100%	**Total Liabilities**	**$201,000**	100%
			Net Worth	**$131,500**	
Cash Inflow			Cash Outflow		
Income			Mortgage or Rent	$15,000	40%
Take Home Pay	$40,000	98%	Car Payment	$3,600	10%
Social Security		0%	Utilities	$4,000	11%
Rental Income		0%	Food/Grocery	$5,000	13%
Interest	$500	1%	Medical	$2,500	7%
Dividends	$500	1%	Travel/Entertain	$3,000	8%
Pensions		0%	Misc	$2,400	6%
Annuities		0%	Automobile Ins	$1,200	3.2%
			Homeowners Ins	$600	1.6%
			Life Ins	$400	1.1%
Total Inflow	**$41,000**	100%	**Total Outflow**	**$37,700**	100%
			Surplus/Deficit	**$3,300**	

Dissecting the net worth statement, on the left side are bank accounts: checking, saving, CDs, etc. Next is personal property, the value of homes, cars, and furnishings. Listed underneath are all liquid investments, stocks, bonds, and mutual funds. Finally, we include the nonliquid assets that won't be accessed until retirement. This includes IRAs (Roth and regular), 401(k), insurance plans, pension plans, and any annuities.

On the right side are all liabilities or anything that is owed. This includes any outstanding mortgages on homes and any vacation property. Next are auto loans, installment payments, and home improvement. Last are unpaid bills including credit cards and personal loans.

If the right side of the balance sheet totals more than the left, it represents a *negative net worth.*

Under normal circumstances, net worth should increase every year. Continuing to pay down a house and saving a little more helps the right side go down and the left side go up. Auto loans can be trickier because while paying off a car it is also depreciating.

In the recent twelve-year span the economy had a couple of periods, 2000–2003 and 2007–2009, where personal net worth declined, even though individuals were saving more and paying down debt. The first period affected individuals who were heavily invested in stocks. The next period took no prisoners as stocks, bonds, and housing all tanked.

What is the importance of preparing a net worth statement? It's always good to know one's worth and total liquidation value. This is an estimate of how much cash one could raise, if necessary. The average person should also know how they're doing financially, if their individual net worth is growing, and at what rate of return. When someone is producing good returns on personal investments, but spends the profits, their net worth can stay flat or even decline. At minimum, an annual review of one's net worth will help aid in making any necessary financial strategy adjustments.

Net Worth versus Financial Assets

The criteria used to determine a person's status as a millionaire has caused controversy. The most common used measurement of net worth counts the total value of all assets owned by a household minus the liabilities.

According to this definition, one would be a millionaire if their household consisted of:

- A paid-off home valued at $800,000
- Furnishings worth $50,000
- Two cars worth $60,000
- Retirement savings account balance of $60,000
- Mutual funds totaling $45,000
- Vacation home worth $325,000 with a $250,000 mortgage
- Automobile loans of $40,000 and $25,000 in credit card debt ($1,340,000 in assets minus $315,000 owed = $1,025,000).

Using a *net financial assets* measurement for determining net worth, equity in a principal residence along with lifestyle assets (cars and furniture) are excluded. From the example, the household would have net financial assets of only $80,000 ($60K retirement plus $45k in mutual funds minus the $25K in credit card debt); the rest of the money is invested in *use* assets.

Another term used is *net investable assets* or working capital. A millionaire is somebody who is free to invest a million units of currency through a broker. During the real estate bubble until 2007, average house prices in some U.S. regions exceeded $1 million, but many homeowners owed large amounts to banks holding the mortgages. Therefore, many people living in million-dollar homes had a net worth far short of a million.

In a study done in 2012 by Business Insider (a business and technology news website), there were only 5.1 million high net worth individuals (HNWI) in the United States, less than 1% of the total population. Admittance to the club requires one million in cash, stocks, or bonds, excluding primary residence and lifestyle assets. That knocks many "pretenders" out of the box who carry significant equity in their main home. If they were to sell, unlocking their equity could put them back in the exclusive club.

What's the bottom line on net worth? The best way to increase true net worth is to concentrate on the right side of the balance sheet. Start with paying off credit cards, since they most likely have the highest interest rate. Next, keep cars longer excluding the need to make additional payments. The final goal is to get the house paid off and then the right side of the balance sheet is clean. After taking control of the liabilities, calculating net worth becomes simple. Just add up all the assets and smile.

If some readers think they don't have enough money to worry about their net worth, they would be wrong. Prior chapters have provided information on managing expenses and investments. Adding a simple worksheet to track those assets and liabilities can be a tool used annually to analyze progress on the road to a better financial future.

Chapter 20

Who Needs to Be a Millionaire?

The housing bubble of 1996–2006 made many people feel like they were finally part of the elite HNWI (high net worth individuals) club. The sense of wealth was fleeting at best and when the bubble burst so did many dreams of early retirement. So the question of who *needs* to be a millionaire should not be confused with who *wants* to be a millionaire.

In the 1990s, many people had their sights set on the *million-dollar number* for retirement. The networks were flooded with commercials showing neighbors asking each other "what's your number?" A book titled *The Millionaire Next Door* came out in 1996 and was all the rage. It did not hurt that it was released during the biggest bull market of the century, helping sell over three million copies. Everyone was looking forward to a new and better future. The markets were in the midst of an eighteen-year (1982–2000) bull run with only a few hiccups along the way. The last ten years of the run, NASDAQ's composite gained an average of 27% each year starting on October 16, 1990, and ending on March 10, 2000. Projections for similar gains going forward made everybody feel wealthy.

Oops, did somebody hear a shoe drop? As readers have learned by now, it would be unlikely for those returns to go on much longer because of regression to the mean. Of course, that's exactly what happened over the following two years as the high-flying NASDAQ dropped over 80%, needing a future gain of 400% just to get back to even.

Financial affluence created by the markets, whether in a retirement account or nonretirement account, is the so-called *wealth effect*. This is an economic term referring to increased spending accompanied by an increase in perceived wealth. Economists in 1968 were baffled when a 10% tax hike failed to slow down consumer spending. The continued spending was later attributed to the wealth effect. While disposable income fell because of increased taxes, asset wealth rose sharply as the stock market moved up. Undaunted, consumers continued their spending spree. Financial experts proved the housing wealth effect is well documented and a standard part of economic theory and modeling. They expect households to continue to consume based on their perceived wealth. Some research estimates that households increase their annual consumption by six cents for every extra dollar of home equity.

All markets, stock, housing etc., have ways of self-correcting. When people get extremely bullish, the market steps in and tempers that enthusiasm. The same happens with net worth, which rises and falls according to the economy. People need to concentrate on lifestyle needs, family situations, health issues, and retirement goals in mapping out a financial journey, not a mythical number.

Financial planners and asset gathering companies such as mutual funds theorize that all retirees need seven figures or a million dollars to retire comfortably. If that's true, only a small percentage of U.S. households will make it to retirement. Maybe the "comfortable" part of retirement has varied definitions.

Believing the recommended need for 80% of preretirement income is necessary in postretirement could scare a small investor into giving up saving. That means someone making $100,000, would need $80,000 to live comfortably in retirement. Facts show that $80,000 was not what individuals or couples were living on. They paid around 25% of that $100k in federal and state taxes, Social Security and Medicare, leaving $75,000. Take away the personal savings, IRAs, or 401(k) that was funded during that period for retirement. Retirees moving to the withdrawal period of their lives could knock off another 10% to 15% or $10,000 to $15,000 not needed for savings.

We now have a more accurate number, $60,000 to $65,000 needed for our mythical individual or couple to live on. Paying off a home will decrease expenses even more. Using $60,000 for living expenses, a couple collecting $42,000 a year in pension and Social Security benefits would need to draw $18,000 each year from retirement accounts, before inflation. A straight draw with no gains or losses over the next twenty years would require $360,000, not a million in retirement savings. Moving to states that have no state income tax or opt not to tax pensions could reduce future tax burdens, adding to the savings.

Everyone's earnings base and spending habits differ. This just explains how to get a handle on future needs. Forget about keeping up with everyone else, including the Joneses. Future retirees should concentrate on managing their own finances, keeping track of assets and liabilities. Lastly, they should define what is needed to live comfortably. Worrying about joining the million-dollar club is a waste of time and energy.

Chapter 21

Getting Retired and Staying Retired

It takes hard work, planning, and maybe some sacrifices to secure a financial goal for retirement. Even after reaching the target, an investor must be vigilant and make adjustments to keep the plan intact. When it comes to the stock market, I previously discussed real returns versus average returns, bull and bear markets, and regression to the mean. Now I would like to tell a retirement tale of a hypothetical investor I call "Lucky Larry."

Larry and his wife had not saved ten cents toward retirement as he was turning forty-four years old; the year was 1982 and the individual retirement account (IRA) was in its infancy. Larry read everything he could about this savings vehicle and found little downside. The government was paying him to save money, since at the time all IRA contributions were tax deductible. The funds invested would not be taxable until withdrawal after age 59½. Funds drawn out before that age are subject to a 10% early withdrawal penalty, with taxes owed on the amount. Since most pensions and early social security benefits do not start until age sixty-two, Uncle Sam's requirements were generous.

Larry invested $2,000 yearly into his IRA with an added $2,000 for his wife. He funded these accounts every January for eighteen consecutive years. His investment of choice was a growth stock fund that mirrored the S&P 500, and for this example, I will use those returns.

In 1989 when the 401(k) retirement plan started to gather momentum, Larry maxed out his 401(k) for the next eleven years including the employer match of the first 3% of his income. Even though his contributions were monthly, to keep things simple I added them as a lump sum at year's end. I did use the actual S&P's returns for those years. Let's see how lucky Larry was.

Larry Invests in the S&P 500

Year	Larry's Starting Balance	Actual S&P Returns	Earnings	Year End Total	New Ira Contr-ibution	401K Contr-ibution	401K 3% Match	Account Totals
1982	**$4,000**	14.80%	$592	$4,592	$4,000			$8,592
1983	$8,592	17.30%	$1,486	$10,078	$4,000			$14,078
1984	$14,078	1.40%	$197	$14,276	$4,000			$18,276
1985	$18,276	26.30%	$4,806	$23,082	$4,000			$27,082
1986	$27,082	14.60%	$3,954	$31,036	$4,000			$35,036
1987	$35,036	2.00%	$701	$35,737	$4,000			$39,737
1988	$39,737	12.40%	$4,927	$44,664	$4,000			$48,664
1989	$48,664	27.30%	$13,285	$61,949	$4,000	$10,000	$1,500	$77,449

Year	Larry's Starting Balance	Actual S&P Returns	Earnings	Year End Total	New Ira Contr-ibution	401K Contr-ibution	401K 3% Match	Account Totals
1990	$77,449	-6.60%	-$5,112	$72,338	$4,000	$10,500	$1,545	$88,383
1991	$88,383	26.30%	$23,245	$111,627	$4,000	$11,000	$1,591	$128,219
1992	$128,219	4.50%	$5,770	$133,988	$4,000	$11,500	$1,639	$151,128
1993	$151,128	7.10%	$10,730	$161,858	$4,000	$12,000	$1,688	$179,546
1994	$179,546	-1.50%	-$2,693	$176,853	$4,000	$12,500	$1,739	$195,092
1995	$195,092	34.10%	$66,526	$261,618	$4,000	$13,000	$1,791	$280,409
1996	$280,409	20.30%	$56,923	$337,332	$4,000	$13,500	$1,845	$356,677
1997	$356,677	31.00%	$110,570	$467,246	$4,000	$14,000	$1,900	$487,147
1998	$487,147	26.70%	$130,068	$617,215	$4,000	$14,500	$1,957	$637,672
1999	$637,672	19.50%	$124,346	$762,018		$15,000	$2,016	**$779,034**
				Totals	$72,000	$137,500	$19,212	
					Total	Invested	$228,712	

Larry invested $228,712 in total: $209,500 was his own money, and $19,212 was the company's match on 3% of his salary. His final balance, not counting dividends reinvested and expense fees, was $779,034.

Had Larry been really lucky he would have bought NASDAQ stocks for the same period, producing much higher returns.

Larry Invests in the NASDAQ

Year	Larry's Starting Balance	Actual NASDAQ Returns	Earnings	Year End Total	New Ira Contr-ibution	401K Contr-ibution	401K 3% Match	Account Totals
1982	**$4,000**	18.70%	$748	$4,748	$4,000			$8,748
1983	$8,748	19.90%	$1,741	$10,489	$4,000			$14,489
1984	$14,489	-11.20%	-$1,623	$12,866	$4,000			$16,866
1985	$16,866	31.40%	$5,296	$22,162	$4,000			$26,162
1986	$26,162	7.50%	$1,962	$28,124	$4,000			$32,124
1987	$32,124	-5.40%	-$1,735	$30,390	$4,000			$34,390
1988	$34,390	15.40%	$5,296	$39,685	$4,000			$43,685

Year	Larry's Starting Balance	Actual NASDAQ Returns	Earnings	Year End Total	New Ira Contr- ibution	401K Contr- ibution	401K 3% Match	Account Totals
1989	$43,685	19.30%	$8,431	$52,117	$4,000	$10,000	$1,500	$67,617
1990	$67,617	-17.80%	-$12,036	$55,581	$4,000	$10,500	$1,545	$71,626
1991	$71,626	56.80%	$40,684	$112,310	$4,000	$11,000	$1,591	$128,901
1992	$128,901	15.50%	$19,980	$148,881	$4,000	$11,500	$1,639	$166,020
1993	$166,020	14.70%	$24,405	$190,425	$4,000	$12,000	$1,688	$208,113
1994	$208,113	-3.20%	-$6,660	$201,453	$4,000	$12,500	$1,739	$219,692
1995	$219,692	39.90%	$87,657	$307,349	$4,000	$13,000	$1,791	$326,140
1996	$326,140	22.70%	$74,034	$400,174	$4,000	$13,500	$1,845	$419,519
1997	$419,519	21.60%	$90,616	$510,135	$4,000	$14,000	$1,900	$530,035
1998	$530,035	39.85%	$211,219	$741,254	$4,000	$14,500	$1,957	$761,711
1999	$761,711	85.60%	$652,025	$1,413,736		$15,000	$2,016	$1,430,752
				Totals	$72,000	$137,500	$19,212	
				Total	Invested	$228,712		

That's not a misprint; a $1,430,752 total return without deducting expenses and trading fees. That is what an extra 3.52% a year will do when compounding over eighteen years, almost double the final total. Isn't hindsight a great thing? Larry sure was a lucky guy catching the biggest bull market of the century. The Dow went from 875 to 11,497, the S&P from 122 to 1,469 and the NASDAQ exploded from 196 to 4,069. The average real return for that period was 15.38% on the Dow, 14.83% on the S&P and 18.35% on the NASDAQ. Those returns for that eighteen-year period may never be repeated, hence the name Lucky Larry.

Let's assume Larry got the S&P returns listed in the previous table. He's now age sixty-two and eligible to draw early social security payments of $1,600 a month or $19,200 a year. His wife also will be getting $1,000 a month or $12,000 a year for a joint total of $31,200 annually. The "experts" claim if retirees withdraw no more than 4% of their retirement money, they will probably outlive their nest egg. Some talking heads claim that if someone's time horizon (cash flow need) is five years or longer, then investing 100% in stocks is necessary to get the growth needed going forward.

Lucky Larry's now retired and decides to follow the pro's advice. He keeps his nest egg in the same S&P 500 fund feeling financially sound knowing the fund had only two losing years in the last eighteen. Following the 4% withdrawal suggestion, Larry and his wife can safely draw out $31,161 or ($779,034 x 4%) each year. With added income of $31,200 from social security, the total of $62,361 is well within their budget. If their investments do half as good as the previous eighteen years, or around 7.4%, then they can draw an extra 3% if needed. Larry loves retirement.

When the new century turned, so did Larry's luck. Following on the next page are two withdrawal scenarios for the next twelve years. In the first, Larry withdrew the $31,161 every year come hell or high water. He decided that's what they needed to live on.

In the second scenario, he withdrew 4% of whatever his current outstanding balance was. By withdrawing a set amount each year, Larry's account balance decreased to $269,228 (65% less) after twelve years. Another eight years of flat or down returns and Larry and his wife would be looking for new careers at age eighty-two, unless they can manage to live only on their combined social security.

Larry withdraws 4% of starting balance every year

Scenario	Ira	Draw	Total	Amount	S&P	Dollar	Account
One	Balance	Rate	With	Left	Return	Gain/ Loss	Balance
2000	**$779,034**	4.00 %	$31,161	$747,872	**-10.14%**	**-$75,834**	$672,038
2001	$672,038		$31,161	$640,877	**-13.19%**	**-$84,532**	$556,346
2002	$556,346		$31,161	$525,185	**-23.37%**	**-$122,736**	$402,449
2003	$402,449		$31,161	$371,288	26.38%	$97,946	$469,234
2004	$469,234		$31,161	$438,073	8.99%	$39,383	$477,455
2005	$477,455		$31,161	$446,294	3.00%	$13,389	$459,683
2006	$459,683		$31,161	$428,522	13.90%	$59,565	$488,087
2007	$488,087		$31,161	$456,926	3.53%	$16,129	$473,055
2008	$473,055		$31,161	$441,894	**-38.49%**	**-$170,085**	$271,809
2009	$271,809		$31,161	$240,648	23.45%	$56,432	$297,080
2010	$297,080		$31,161	$265,919	12.78%	$33,984	$299,904
2011	$299,904		$31,161	$268,743	0.00%	$0	$268,743
2012	$268,743		$31,161	$237,582	13.32%	$31,646	**$269,228**
	Amount	Drawn	**$405,093**				

Larry withdraws 4% of remaining balance

Scenario	Ira	Draw	Total	Amount	S&P	Dollar	Account
Two	Balance	Rate	With	Left	Return	Gain/ Loss	Balance
2000	**$779,034**	4.00 %	$31,161	$747,872	**-10.14%**	**-$75,834**	$672,038
2001	$672,038	4.00%	$26,882	$645,157	**-13.19%**	**-$85,096**	$560,061
2002	$560,061	4.00%	$22,402	$537,658	**-23.37%**	**-$125,651**	$412,007
2003	$412,007	4.00%	$16,480	$395,527	26.38%	$104,340	$499,867
2004	$499,867	4.00%	$19,995	$479,872	8.99%	$43,141	$523,013
2005	$523,013	4.00%	$20,921	$502,092	3.00%	$15,063	$517,155
2006	$517,155	4.00%	$20,686	$496,469	13.90%	$69,009	$565,478
2007	$565,478	4.00%	$22,619	$542,859	3.53%	$19,163	$562,022
2008	$562,022	4.00%	$22,481	$539,541	**-38.49%**	**-$207,669**	**$331,872**
2009	$331,872	4.00%	$13,275	$318,597	23.45%	$74,711	$393,308
2010	$393,308	4.00%	$15,732	$377,576	12.78%	$48,254	$425,830
2011	$425,830	4.00%	$17,033	$408,797	0.00%	$0	$408,797
2012	$408,797	4.00%	$16,352	$392,445	13.32%	$52,274	**$444,718**
	Amount	Drawn	**$266,019**				

In the second example, Larry's retirement account balance is down *only* 43% to $444,718 over the same period. This result was because he withdrew $139,074 less ($405,093 minus $266,019). By the year 2012 Larry's drawing out $16,352 per year, little more than one-half the amount he needs to live on. Larry has to either find another way to supplement his lost retirement income, or cut expenses.

Now let's look at the REALLY Lucky Larry who invested in NASDAQ's stocks. He was feeling good with $1,430,752 in his retirement account, and withdrew a set amount of $57,230 (4%) of the starting balance. That's an extra $26,069 a year over the S&P 500 scenario. They didn't consider themselves rich living on $88,430 a year (withdrawals and social security), but life was good for a while. By 2013, Larry's retirement account was almost out of money, even though he only withdrew $743,990. "Mr. Market" got the rest of it ($653,643). Four big down years (2000, 2001, 2002, and 2008) played havoc on the finances he so diligently built up over the prior eighteen years.

Larry withdraws 4% of starting balance every year

Year	Ira Balance	Draw Rate	Total	Amount Left	NASDAQ Return	Dollar Gain/Loss	Account Balance
2000	**$1,430,752**	4.00%	$57,230	$1,373,522	**-39.30%**	**-$539,794**	$833,728
2001	$833,728		$57,230	$776,498	**-21.10%**	**-$163,841**	$612,657
2002	$612,657		$57,230	$555,427	**-31.50%**	**-$174,959**	$380,467
2003	$380,467		$57,230	$323,237	50.00%	$161,619	$484,856
2004	$484,856		$57,230	$427,626	8.60%	$36,776	$464,402
2005	$464,402		$57,230	$407,172	1.40%	$5,700	$412,872
2006	$412,872		$57,230	$355,642	9.50%	$33,786	$389,428
2007	$389,428		$57,230	$332,198	9.80%	$32,555	$364,754
2008	$364,754		$57,230	$307,524	**-40.50%**	**-$124,547**	$182,977
2009	$182,977		$57,230	$125,747	43.90%	$55,203	$180,950
2010	$180,950		$57,230	$123,720	16.90%	$20,909	$144,628
2011	$144,628		$57,230	$87,398	**-1.80%**	**-$1,573**	$85,825
2012	$85,825		$57,230	$28,595	15.82%	$4,524	**$33,119**
	Amount	**Drawn**	**$743,990**				

It's obvious Larry hadn't known, as the reader now knows, periods of outperformance are followed by periods of underperformance. The market has shown the longer and more severe the outperformance, the longer and more severe the underperformance. That's how we regress to the mean. Larry could have slowed the bleeding by withdrawing 4% of the outstanding balance. Nevertheless, even by the third year (2002), his withdrawal amount of $25,260 would be under what he believed necessary and his balance would be down over $1,000,000 to $415,274.

Larry withdraws 4% of remaining balance

Year	Ira Balance	Draw Rate	Total Withdrawal	Amount Left	NASDAQ Return	Dollar Gain/Loss	Account Balance
2000	$1,430,752	4.00%	$57,230	$1,373,522	-39.30%	-$539,794	$833,728
2001	$833,728	4.00%	$33,349	$800,379	-21.10%	-$168,880	$631,499
2002	$631,499	4.00%	$25,260	$606,239	-31.50%	-$190,965	$415,274
2003	$415,274	4.00%	$16,611	$398,663	50.00%	$199,331	$597,994
2004	$597,994	4.00%	$23,920	$574,074	8.60%	$49,370	$623,445
2005	$623,445	4.00%	$24,938	$598,507	1.40%	$8,379	$606,886
2006	$606,886	4.00%	$24,275	$582,611	9.50%	$55,348	$637,959
2007	$637,959	4.00%	$25,518	$612,440	9.80%	$60,019	$672,459
2008	$672,459	4.00%	$26,898	$645,561	-40.50%	-$261,452	$384,109
2009	$384,109	4.00%	$15,364	$368,744	43.90%	$161,879	$530,623
2010	$530,623	4.00%	$21,225	$509,398	16.90%	$86,088	$595,487
2011	$595,487	4.00%	$23,819	$571,667	-1.80%	-$10,290	$561,377
2012	$561,377	4.00%	$22,455	$538,922	15.82%	$85,257	$624,180
	Amount	Drawn	$340,864				

So what should poor Larry have done after riding the biggest bull market in history to extraordinary gains? If his IRA investment choice was the NASDAQ, I hope he also explored long-term market trends. Based on the concept of regression to the mean, he might have considered selling his stocks.

William Bernstein, author of the *Four Pillars of Investing*, takes it a step further declaring the worst investing mistake is not knowing when to take your money off the table. He wrote a good article about this issue in *Money Magazine* (September 2012). The basic premise is if an investor were lucky enough to have won the investing game like Larry did, then they don't have to play anymore.

Let's check out how Larry would have fared if he took his gains and cashed out investing in bonds or CDs during the same period.

Larry cashes out his S&P 500 & withdraws 4%

Year	Ira Balance	Draw Rate	Total With	Amount Left	Mix Bonds/Cds	Dollar Gain/Loss	Account Balance
2000	**$779,034**	4.00%	$31,161	$747,872	5.00%	$37,394	$785,266
2001	$785,266	4.00%	$31,411	$753,855	5.00%	$37,693	$791,548
2002	$791,548	4.00%	$31,662	$759,886	5.00%	$37,994	$797,881
2003	$797,881	4.00%	$31,915	$765,965	5.00%	$38,298	$804,264
2004	$804,264	4.00%	$32,171	$772,093	5.00%	$38,605	$810,698
2005	$810,698	4.00%	$32,428	$778,270	5.00%	$38,913	$817,183
2006	$817,183	4.00%	$32,687	$784,496	5.00%	$39,225	$823,721
2007	$823,721	4.00%	$32,949	$790,772	4.00%	$31,631	$822,403
2008	$822,403	4.00%	$32,896	$789,507	4.00%	$31,580	$821,087
2009	$821,087	4.00%	$32,843	$788,244	4.00%	$31,530	$819,773
2010	$819,773	4.00%	$32,791	$786,982	3.00%	$23,609	$810,592
2011	$810,592	4.00%	$32,424	$778,168	3.00%	$23,345	$801,513
2012	$801,513	4.00%	$32,061	$769,453	3.00%	$23,084	**$792,536**
	Amount	Drawn	$419,399				

Larry's 4% withdrawals increased slightly and his ending balance was still higher than his initial bond or CD (certificate of deposit) investment twelve years later. I blended a CD and bond rate over the last twelve-year period.

Had he been lucky enough to ride the NASDAQ bull and dismounted at retirement, he would forever been known as "Larry the Legend." Same scenario only better, Larry withdraws an extra $26,000 per year and never runs out of money. Sweet! If Larry had any heirs, either way they would love him.

A couple of conditions: To keep the math simple, I did not consider any fund or stock trading expenses nor did I count reinvesting any dividends. Since the dividend rate was low during that period (1%–2%), those two probably canceled each other out. Second, I wanted to show the best-case scenario followed by a worst case.

Larry cashes out his NASDAQ totals-withdraws 4% of balance

Year	Ira Balance	Draw Rate	Total Draw	Amount Left	Bonds Cds	Dollar Gain/Loss	Account Balance
2000	$1,430,752	4.00%	$57,230	$1,373,522	5.00%	$68,676	$1,442,198
2001	$1,442,198	4.00%	$57,688	$1,384,510	5.00%	$69,226	$1,453,736
2002	$1,453,736	4.00%	$58,149	$1,395,586	5.00%	$69,779	$1,465,366
2003	$1,465,366	4.00%	$58,615	$1,406,751	5.00%	$70,338	$1,477,089
2004	$1,477,089	4.00%	$59,084	$1,418,005	5.00%	$70,900	$1,488,905
2005	$1,488,905	4.00%	$59,556	$1,429,349	5.00%	$71,467	$1,500,817
2006	$1,500,817	4.00%	$60,033	$1,440,784	5.00%	$72,039	$1,512,823
2007	$1,512,823	4.00%	$60,513	$1,452,310	4.00%	$58,092	$1,510,403
2008	$1,510,403	4.00%	$60,416	$1,449,987	4.00%	$57,999	$1,507,986
2009	$1,507,986	4.00%	$60,319	$1,447,667	4.00%	$57,907	$1,505,573
2010	$1,505,573	4.00%	$60,223	$1,445,350	3.00%	$43,361	$1,488,711
2011	$1,488,711	4.00%	$59,548	$1,429,162	3.00%	$42,875	$1,472,037
2012	$1,472,037	4.00%	$58,881	$1,413,156	3.00%	$42,395	$1,455,550
	Amount	Drawn	$770,256				

Just for the record, I did not fit Larry's time frame to capture the exact bottom and top of the bull market. Nobody can call the precise bottoms and tops for bull or bear markets. Nobody! In fact the Dow peaked out at 11,722 in January 2001, the S&P 500 at 1,526 in late March 2001 and the NASDAQ also peaked in March at 5,048, almost 1,000 points or 20% higher. I just used the period from 1982 through 1999.

Most investors will not get 100% of any bull market. However, baby boomers born after 1946 had 1982 through 1999 available to capitalize on. From 1966 to 1982, the markets were flat and due for an extended period of outperformance. A prudent investor at retirement should consider cutting back his or her exposure to stocks. The adage is 100 minus your age for a total stock allocation. That would leave Larry only 38% invested in stocks and the rest in cash and bonds at retirement, cushioning the blow of the bear market.

Following long-term cycles gives an investor a better chance to take advantage of the longer bull trends and be cautious when the unavoidable long bear markets appear. It will also help one temper the enthusiasm that drives the markets and investors to extremes.

Chapter 22

Putting It All Together, Improving the Bottom Line

The previous chapters in this book touched on areas in one's life that have financial impact. Whether individuals are saving for a specific future goal, investing for retirement, or just trying to get the maximum benefit out of their paycheck, I hope readers picked up enough information to improve their status quo.

The obvious way to increase personal financial standing, besides inheritance, is to create more income than expense. The wider the gap becomes, the greater the rate of increase in wealth. Simple as it sounds, making it happen is not as apparent. Consider the fact a person or couple averaging $50,000 a year in salary, and working from ages twenty-five to sixty-five will gross *$2,000,000*. After deducting around 25% for taxes including social security and Medicare, that still leaves $1.5 million in earned income. That does not include any potential interest earned on any savings or investments. Most people busy with life's day-to-day problems do not dwell on the ultimate big financial picture and the potential it provides.

So what happened to all that money? Below a certain income level, everything is spent on everyday living, with nothing left over for savings. Others spend with exuberance, not worrying about tomorrow. Some will be able to find a balance between the two. Various ways to improve one's financial bottom line has been the focus of this book.

What has not been discussed is the abyss of credit card debt. It's simple: People should not spend more than they make. Just because the government does it, does not mean its constituents should. We don't have a personal debt ceiling we can vote away. There is no problem with well-managed credit for ease of handling financial transactions. Rule One: Fully pay off each month's credit card bill. Rule Two: If rule number one can't be followed, then a credit card should only be used for emergencies. Once someone has mortgaged the future for the present through debt, it is hard to get out.

Saving in itself is not a sure way to increase one's wealth if personal liability continues to rise at the same pace. Mortgage debt is likely unavoidable, but can be deducted off most federal and state taxes. However, as covered in Chapter 8, "The Refinance Trap," extending the life of a mortgage for lower current payments may not be the best financial decision unless specifically saving the payment difference. Many poor financial decisions are based on instant gratification, the "live for today" mind-set. We want *things* now: the bigger, the better, the fastest, the latest technology, the newest models, and that elusive shot at winning free money.

To emphasize the practical applications of prior chapters, following are two different hypothetical financial situations. We will review the habits and lifestyles of two couples at different stages in their lives, and see how they can change the disposition of their bottom lines.

Bill and Susan

According to the 2010 census bureau data, there were over 58 million married couples in the United States and almost 27 million, or 46%, are without children (including empty nesters). I Googled it so it must be true! Bill and Susan are typical DINKS (dual income, no kids). They are married and in their early thirties. They have not started saving for retirement, but figure they still have plenty of time with thirty-some years of work remaining. Their current combined income totals $53,000 a year. Bill earns $32,000 with Susan's $21,000 ranking them above the 2011 national average of $50,054. They look forward to their yearly average tax return of roughly $2,800. The money is spent on big-ticket items or a dream vacation. They do have a cash value life insurance policy they bought instead of a retirement plan or IRA. A guilty pleasure of theirs is spending $20 a week on the Lotto just because "somebody has to win." Bill has yet to contribute to his 401(k), an actual retirement plan, which has a 3% matching contribution.

Incorporating some of the previous chapter's ideas into their financial framework illustrates how to increase the bottom line, without having to save any extra money. Sounds like an impossibly tall task, but it can be accomplished just by embracing wiser spending habits.

First, Bill and Susan need to take the $1,040 (52 x $20) per year spent on Lotto tickets and put that aside per Chapter 1. The next step is to adjust their federal withholding and try to come as close to a zero balance owed at tax time, as explained in Chapter 4, "Tax Refund: Spend or Save?" This can be done by using the withholding calculator at www.irs.gov. Breaking even at tax time can be an art rather than a science and may take some practice. Between the lottery and tax refund money, Bill and Susan now have $3,900 per year available for investing. With this new disposable income of around $75 a week, $55 less in federal withholding and $20 a week from the Lotto, they can invest in a 401(k) plan and/or an individual IRA.

Bill can start contributing 6% of his income or $1,920 into his 401(k) ($32,000 x 6%) also receiving a $960 match, for a total of $2,880. That leaves around $2,000 for Susan to start up an individual IRA. Both the 401(k) and the IRA are fully tax deductible so they would realize an extra $588 in tax savings at their 15% top bracket ($3,920 x 15%). Even though they withheld only enough taxes in an attempt to break even, they will still end up getting a smaller refund, thanks to their retirement contributions. This refund can be their "mad money," paying themselves for being financially astute.

To recap, Bill and Susan made two changes; they stopped playing the Lotto and saved their extra withholding, investing both into retirement accounts. They do not get to splurge at tax time, but will still get a refund. They also have other ways to save by keeping their autos longer (Chapter 2). Cheaper term insurance can replace a whole life policy, if not needed for estate purposes (Chapter 5).

The couple now has $4,880 to invest for the long-term, the original $3,920, plus Bill's company match of $960 (free money). With a potential thirty years until retirement, it would be to their advantage to invest in stocks. In Chapter 18, "Where to Invest," I tracked a recent thirty-three-year span to get some idea of how the different indices fared. There are no guarantees for the next thirty-three-years because we know that long-term averages do regress to the mean (Chapter 15). However, the tracked period did have three major sell-offs in 1987, 2000 to 2002, and 2008 to 2009 and still posted decent returns overall.

If Bill and Susan invest $4,880 or around $400 per month for thirty years and get an 8% return net of fees and expenses, they would have around $605,000 at retirement, tax deferred. I used the lowest real return for the eight indices (S&P 8.11%) also from Chapter 18, and assumed they shopped around for the lowest fees covered in Chapter 17, "Expenses Do Matter."

Using the Russell 2000's last thirty-three-year real return of 12%, net of fees, and calculated over thirty-years, the total investment is an astounding

$1,411,966. I proofed out the work in Appendices E and F for any skeptics. I used 8% yearly or .667% monthly S&P returns; and 12% for the yearly or 1% for the monthly rate for the Russell Small Cap.

Tom and Ann

Tom and Ann are the opposite of Bill and Susan. They are mid-forties and already raised two children, who both just graduated college. Their retirement period is twenty years and so far, they have managed to save $40,000 in an IRA. Tom has a good job and makes about $80,000. Ann recently found something part-time in the $20,000 range to add some extra income. A refinanced mortgage on their home still has twenty years left. They lease both cars and are thinking of buying a time-share now that the kids are gone. Tom and Ann do not have the extra ten years of compounding that Bill and Susan did, but there is still plenty of time and investing dollars to get decent results.

A good place for this couple to start is Chapter 2, "Automobiles: Lease or Buy?" Depending on what they drive, there could be a potential $17,500 in savings per car over the next twenty-one years. They need to stop leasing; instead buy and hold their cars on average for seven years. Using the proper negotiation tactics in Chapter 3, "Car Buying," could even save them a little more.

They might reconsider buying a time-share after reading Chapter 6, "Time-Shares: Vacations, Not Investments." The facts being time-shares are marked up 50%, the payback period is about fifteen years, and they depreciate rapidly. This couple should consider less costly vacation options.

If Tom and Ann would like to retire with their home paid off, refinancing again is not advisable. They're getting closer to paying more toward the principal and less toward the interest (Chapter 8, "The Refinance Trap"). It's a good time to think about paying extra each month to accelerate their payoff. That money comes right off the principal, knocking a few more years off the twenty-one years remaining.

The maximum individual IRA contribution in 2012 was $5,500 with an extra $1,000 after age 50. Tom decides to invest $5,500 until retirement and Ann adds $2,500 to the mix for a total of $8,000 each year or $667 per month added to his or her original $40,000 savings. Withstanding any financial emergencies, this should not be an insurmountable amount, if incorporating Susan's new income and any potential savings from changing their car leasing habits. Using the same 8% rate of return, Tom and Ann could have $596,125 amassed by retirement.

Tom and Ann had to make more significant lifestyle changes and invest more aggressively for the twenty years prior to retirement. With ten years less of compounding and saving almost twice as much ($8,000 versus $3,920) than Bill and Susan, Tom and Ann's nest egg still falls short by $8,875 ($605,000 to $596,125). By using the Russell's return of 12%, Tom and Ann could have a final balance of $1,102,134. Note this still does not meet Bill and Susan's optimal total of

$1,411,966, but it is still a respectable bottom line. (See Appendices G and H)

Chapter 15, "Calling a 'Fowl' on Financial Black Swans," explained how using past returns does not guarantee future results. Some savers like Lucky Larry in Chapter 21, "Getting Retired and Staying Retired," will hit a sweet spot in their investing cycle. He was able to use that luck and his financial resources to take advantage of those circumstances. Others will not be so lucky and their returns will underperform the long-term averages. To be on the safer side, investors must always assume they will not get the best-case scenario. To compensate for that, one should always save a little more of their original income.

I hope these twenty-two chapters have given some good solid information, both in general knowledge and for financial investing. I don't expect all the chapters to be viable options for everyone. I do hope younger readers see the wisdom in building a solid financial strategy early on in their lives. Regardless of age or income, I am optimistic any reader now has the knowledge base to improve their bottom line. After all, don't you want your money to work harder for you?

Epilogue

Crossroads

I am confident that readers of this book will pick up a few new tips on making the road to financial security or retirement a bit easier. If already retired, then maybe I was able to "teach an old dog some new tricks." I tried not to get too preachy, as one person's priorities may be as high on another person's list. At times I alluded to the mistakes my wife and I had made and other times you had to read between the lines.

There will always be financial crossroads that individuals wander upon in their lives. We will never know for sure if we followed the best path. Everyone, at some point, looks back and tries to second-guess what could have happened had different choices been made. That's why *they* say, "Hindsight is 20/20." Mistakes and misjudgments will be part of everyone's financial roadmap to the future. That's how we learn, enrich our lives, and become who we are.

My wife and I were lucky enough to come to one of our financial crossroads early in life and I believe we chose the right path. Here is a personal story about a red 944 Porsche that changed everything. In January 1982, we had been married for a little over four years, saving about $2,000 a year or $8,000. I *needed* to buy another car but *wanted* the new 944, dubbed "the poor man's Porsche" because it cost under $20,000. That was still a lot of money in those days. Also attached would be higher insurance premiums and probably a few speeding tickets.

Coincidentally, 1982 was the birth of the IRA. Here was our dilemma, put $8,000 down on the Porsche and have a really sweet ride with a hefty car payment, *or* look for a cheaper car and start investing in an IRA. As I mentioned in a previous chapter the IRA option was a "no brainer." We decided to put $2,000 apiece in our own IRA accounts and the remaining $4,000 down on a new 1982 Plymouth Sapporo, Mitsubishi's forerunner to the Gallant. The car cost $7,900 leaving us with a small car payment, enabling us to fund our IRAs going forward. From investing in IRAs, we moved on to a 401(k), and finally started saving in tax-free Roth IRAs in the late '90s. Twenty-three years later in 2005, we both decided to retire early. We caught most of the 1982 to 1999 bull market and were fortunate enough to avoid the severe downturn from 2000 to 2003. The information I covered in Chapter 15, "regression to the mean," came in handy. The fate of Lucky Larry in the

"Staying Retired" chapter helped put our longer view of retirement in perspective.

Some of the other chapters in this book, "Where to Invest" and "Expenses Do Matter," did not come into play for us until I starting doing the research and writing this book. It helped this *old dog* learn something new. I call that a win-win for everybody, reader and author.

Early retirement is not everybody's cup of tea. Some people never adjust to the change and it may do them no service to get out of the game early. Others continue to work as long as physically possible and there is nothing wrong with that choice either. Warren Buffet comes to mind as someone who has stayed active into his eighties. My goal has been to help guide readers in navigating their personal journeys through the investing maze to a more secure financial future. Everyone must make the choices based on their personal goals and avoid the "one-size-fits-all" investing plans. I hope this book will continue to be a source of reference in mapping your financial future. It doesn't make any difference if your life leads you down the expressways or back roads, only you can choose to help your money work harder for you.

Acknowledgments

In my first book, *By a Nose: Gambling Tales from a Horseracing Insider,* I think I thanked everybody up to and including my garbage man. I didn't want to leave anybody out. Now that I have been "around the track" once and have gone from telling gambling stories to personal finance strategies, I think I can narrow down my kudos.

First, I have to thank my two muses, Marilyn Nardin, my sister-in-law, and Steve Johns, longtime friend. I knew they would review my writing from different perspectives and have opposite views, but if both understood what I was trying to say, then I knew I might be on to something. I sent them each a chapter or two at a time over a three-month period and their feedback and suggestions helped shape the finished product.

Marilyn thought this book would be a great Christmas gift for our nieces and nephews. Steve hoped I would finish in time for his wife Laurie to read in advance of her upcoming retirement. Steve also was instrumental in honing in on the best title, making him a perfect two for two. I probably wouldn't have gotten very far if they hadn't hung with me in the early chapters. Many thanks to you both for sticking with it.

I would like to thank my nephew Patrick Dominguez and his wife Veronica for literally stripping down the barriers and providing a great arm shot for a compelling book cover. Speaking of the cover, thanks to Bill Cole (another nephew) for doing a phenomenal job using his graphic design talents and turning the artistic concept locked in our heads into an original book cover. Check out his unique talents at billcoledesign.com.

I informed my cousin Teresa Brinati I was thinking of writing another book and told her I didn't want to impose again, after all the hard work she put in on the first one. Instead, I asked her to recommend some style writing programs that I might find useful. Once again, she willingly volunteered to be a part of the writing process providing her expertise. Her only wish this time was to have the manuscript sent all at once, not piecemeal. That worked out better for me because I gave myself a four-month writing deadline. I completed a rough draft on April Fools' Day. Coincidence?

I always knew Teresa was a wordsmith wonder and I have now discovered she's also a punctuation pro and an erudite editor. Teresa, with your suggestions and never-ending support you have become my literary lioness keeping this project and me on track. I don't want to say you're my favorite cousin, but really . . . . Thanks again for all the help.

I have saved the best for last. When I told my wife Jerri that I was going to write another book, her first response was, "Been there, done that." She worked tirelessly rewriting *By a Nose*, so I couldn't blame her for opting out.

After constant pleading, she volunteered to write the foreword for this book. Before writing anything, she needed to read some chapters to get a sense of where I was headed. A month later, she was onboard and immersed in rewrites. I think we may have spent twice as much time rewriting as I spent writing the original draft. You know how after being with someone long enough you can finish each other's sentences. Apparently, that works in writing, too! The cover concept was also her idea (with thumbs up from Marilyn) and that turned out terrific. Jerri, you made this book a reality for me and I cannot thank you enough.

Quoting from my favorite rock band, AC/DC:

"For those about to rock [I] salute you."

Appendix A (Chapter 12)
Calculating Dow Jones Real Rate of Return

Date	Starting Payment	Real Rate Of Return	Interest	Total	Next Payment
1982	$4,000	19.6%	$784	$4,784	$4,000
1983	$8,784	20.3%	$1,783	$10,567	$4,000
1984	$14,567	-3.7%	($539)	$14,028	$4,000
1985	$18,028	27.7%	$4,994	$23,022	$4,000
1986	$27,022	22.6%	$6,107	$33,129	$4,000
1987	$37,129	2.3%	$854	$37,983	$4,000
1988	$41,983	11.8%	$4,954	$46,937	$4,000
1989	$50,937	27.0%	$13,753	$64,690	$4,000
1990	$68,690	-4.3%	($2,954)	$65,736	$4,000
1991	$69,736	20.3%	$14,156	$83,893	$4,000
1992	$87,893	4.2%	$3,691	$91,584	$4,000
1993	$95,584	13.7%	$13,095	$108,679	$4,000
1994	$112,679	2.1%	$2,366	$115,045	$4,000
1995	$119,045	33.5%	$39,880	$158,926	$4,000
1996	$162,926	26.0%	$42,361	$205,286	$4,000
1997	$209,286	22.6%	$47,299	$256,585	$4,000
1998	$260,585	16.1%	$41,954	$302,539	$4,000
1999	$306,539	25.2%	$77,248	$383,787	$4,000
2000	$387,787	-6.2%	($24,043)	$363,744	$4,000
2001	$367,744	-7.1%	($26,110)	$341,634	$4,000
2002	$345,634	-16.8%	($57,928)	$287,706	$4,000
2003	$291,706	25.3%	$73,860	$365,566	$4,000
2004	$369,566	3.1%	$11,457	$381,023	$4,000
2005	$385,023	-0.6%	($2,310)	$382,712	$4,000
2006	$386,712	16.3%	$62,841	$449,553	$4,000
2007	$453,553	6.4%	$28,937	$482,490	$4,000
2008	$486,490	-33.8%	($164,628)	$321,862	$4,000
2009	$325,862	18.8%	$61,327	$387,189	$4,000
2010	$391,189	11.0%	$43,109	$434,298	$4,000
2011	$438,298	5.5%	$24,238	$462,536	$4,000
2012	$466,536	7.2%	$33,637	$500,173	
	Total	**316.1%**			
	# of Years	**31**		**Investment**	**$124,000**
	Simple Rate	**10.2%**	**Real Rate**	**7.7%**	

Appendix A (Chapter 12) con't
Calculating Dow Jones Simple Rate of 10.2%

Year	Starting Payment	3Simple Rate	Interest	Total	Next Payment
1982	$4,000	10.2%	$408	$4,408	$4,000
1983	$8,408	10.2%	$857	$9,264	$4,000
1984	$13,264	10.2%	$1,352	$14,616	$4,000
1985	$18,616	10.2%	$1,897	$20,513	$4,000
1986	$24,513	10.2%	$2,498	$27,011	$4,000
1987	$31,011	10.2%	$3,160	$34,171	$4,000
1988	$38,171	10.2%	$3,890	$42,060	$4,000
1989	$46,060	10.2%	$4,694	$50,754	$4,000
1990	$54,754	10.2%	$5,579	$60,333	$4,000
1991	$64,333	10.2%	$6,556	$70,889	$4,000
1992	$74,889	10.2%	$7,631	$82,520	$4,000
1993	$86,520	10.2%	$8,816	$95,337	$4,000
1994	$99,337	10.2%	$10,122	$109,459	$4,000
1995	$113,459	10.2%	$11,561	$125,020	$4,000
1996	$129,020	10.2%	$13,147	$142,168	$4,000
1997	$146,168	10.2%	$14,894	$161,062	$4,000
1998	$165,062	10.2%	$16,820	$181,882	$4,000
1999	$185,882	10.2%	$18,941	$204,823	$4,000
2000	$208,823	10.2%	$21,279	$230,102	$4,000
2001	$234,102	10.2%	$23,855	$257,957	$4,000
2002	$261,957	10.2%	$26,693	$288,651	$4,000
2003	$292,651	10.2%	$29,821	$322,472	$4,000
2004	$326,472	10.2%	$33,267	$359,739	$4,000
2005	$363,739	10.2%	$37,065	$400,805	$4,000
2006	$404,805	10.2%	$41,250	$446,054	$4,000
2007	$450,054	10.2%	$45,861	$495,915	$4,000
2008	$499,915	10.2%	$50,941	$550,856	$4,000
2009	$554,856	10.2%	$56,540	$611,396	$4,000
2010	$615,396	10.2%	$62,709	$678,105	$4,000
2011	$682,105	10.2%	$69,506	$751,611	$4,000
2012	$755,611	10.2%	$76,997	$832,608	
Total				**Investment**	**$124,000**

Appendix A (Chapter 12) con't
Calculating the S&P 500 Real Rate of Return

Year	Starting Payment	Real Rate Of Return	Interest	Total	Next Payment
1982	$4,000	14.8%	$592	$4,592	$4,000
1983	$8,592	17.3%	$1,486	$10,078	$4,000
1984	$14,078	1.4%	$197	$14,276	$4,000
1985	$18,276	26.3%	$4,806	$23,082	$4,000
1986	$27,082	14.6%	$3,954	$31,036	$4,000
1987	$35,036	2.0%	$701	$35,737	$4,000
1988	$39,737	12.4%	$4,927	$44,664	$4,000
1989	$48,664	27.3%	$13,285	$61,949	$4,000
1990	$65,949	**-6.6%**	($4,353)	$61,597	$4,000
1991	$65,597	26.3%	$17,252	$82,849	$4,000
1992	$86,849	4.5%	$3,908	$90,757	$4,000
1993	$94,757	7.1%	$6,728	$101,484	$4,000
1994	$105,484	**-1.5%**	($1,582)	$103,902	$4,000
1995	$107,902	34.1%	$36,795	$144,697	$4,000
1996	$148,697	20.3%	$30,185	$178,882	$4,000
1997	$182,882	31.0%	$56,694	$239,576	$4,000
1998	$243,576	26.7%	$65,035	$308,611	$4,000
1999	$312,611	19.5%	$60,959	$373,570	$4,000
2000	$377,570	**-10.1%**	($38,135)	$339,435	$4,000
2001	$343,435	**-13.0%**	($44,647)	$298,789	$4,000
2002	$302,789	**-23.4%**	($70,762)	$232,027	$4,000
2003	$236,027	26.4%	$62,264	$298,291	$4,000
2004	$302,291	9.0%	$27,206	$329,497	$4,000
2005	$333,497	3.0%	$10,005	$343,502	$4,000
2006	$347,502	13.6%	$47,260	$394,762	$4,000
2009	$398,762	3.5%	$14,076	$412,838	$4,000
2008	$416,838	**-38.5%**	($160,441)	$256,397	$4,000
2009	$260,397	23.5%	$61,063	$321,460	$4,000
2010	$325,460	12.8%	$41,594	$367,054	$4,000
2011	$371,054	0.0%	$0	$371,054	$4,000
2012	$375,054	13.3%	$49,957	$425,011	
Total	**Total**	**297.6%**		**Investment**	**$124,000**
	Years	**31**			
	Simple Rate	**9.6%**	**Real Rate**	**6.9%**	

Appendix A (Chapter 12) con't
Calculating S&P 500 Simple Rate of 9.6%

Year	Starting Payment	Simple Rate Of Return	Interest	Total	Next Payment
1982	$4,000	9.6%	$384	$4,384	$4,000
1983	$8,384	9.6%	$805	$9,189	$4,000
1984	$13,189	9.6%	$1,266	$14,455	$4,000
1985	$18,455	9.6%	$1,772	$20,227	$4,000
1986	$24,227	9.6%	$2,326	$26,552	$4,000
1987	$30,552	9.6%	$2,933	$33,485	$4,000
1988	$37,485	9.6%	$3,599	$41,084	$4,000
1989	$45,084	9.6%	$4,328	$49,412	$4,000
1990	$53,412	9.6%	$5,128	$58,540	$4,000
1991	$62,540	9.6%	$6,004	$68,544	$4,000
1992	$72,544	9.6%	$6,964	$79,508	$4,000
1993	$83,508	9.6%	$8,017	$91,524	$4,000
1994	$95,524	9.6%	$9,170	$104,695	$4,000
1995	$108,695	9.6%	$10,435	$119,129	$4,000
1996	$123,129	9.6%	$11,820	$134,950	$4,000
1997	$138,950	9.6%	$13,339	$152,289	$4,000
1998	$156,289	9.6%	$15,004	$171,293	$4,000
1999	$175,293	9.6%	$16,828	$192,121	$4,000
2000	$196,121	9.6%	$18,828	$214,949	$4,000
2001	$218,949	9.6%	$21,019	$239,968	$4,000
2002	$243,968	9.6%	$23,421	$267,389	$4,000
2003	$271,389	9.6%	$26,053	$297,442	$4,000
2004	$301,442	9.6%	$28,938	$330,380	$4,000
2005	$334,380	9.6%	$32,101	$366,481	$4,000
2006	$370,481	9.6%	$35,566	$406,047	$4,000
2008	$410,047	9.6%	$39,365	$449,411	$4,000
2008	$453,411	9.6%	$43,527	$496,939	$4,000
2009	$500,939	9.6%	$48,090	$549,029	$4,000
2010	$553,029	9.6%	$53,091	$606,120	$4,000
2011	$610,120	9.6%	$58,572	$668,691	$4,000
2012	$672,691	9.6%	$64,578	$737,270	
Total		**9.6%**		**Investment**	**$124,000**

Appendix A (Chapter 12) con't
Calculating NASDAQ Real Rate of Return

Year	Starting Payment	Real Rate Of Return	Interest	Total	Next Payment
1982	$4,000	18.7%	$748	$4,748	$4,000
1983	$8,748	19.9%	$1,741	$10,489	$4,000
1984	$14,489	-11.2%	($1,623)	$12,866	$4,000
1985	$16,866	31.4%	$5,296	$22,162	$4,000
1986	$26,162	7.4%	$1,936	$28,098	$4,000
1987	$32,098	-5.3%	($1,701)	$30,397	$4,000
1988	$34,397	15.4%	$5,297	$39,694	$4,000
1989	$43,694	19.3%	$8,433	$52,127	$4,000
1990	$56,127	-17.8%	($9,991)	$46,136	$4,000
1991	$50,136	56.8%	$28,477	$78,614	$4,000
1992	$82,614	15.5%	$12,805	$95,419	$4,000
1993	$99,419	14.8%	$14,714	$114,133	$4,000
1994	$118,133	-3.2%	($3,780)	$114,353	$4,000
1995	$118,353	39.9%	$47,223	$165,575	$4,000
1996	$169,575	22.7%	$38,494	$208,069	$4,000
1997	$212,069	21.6%	$45,807	$257,876	$4,000
1998	$261,876	39.6%	$103,703	$365,579	$4,000
1999	$369,579	85.6%	$316,359	$685,938	$4,000
2000	$689,938	-39.3%	($271,146)	$418,792	$4,000
2001	$422,792	-21.1%	($89,209)	$333,583	$4,000
2002	$337,583	-31.5%	($106,440)	$231,143	$4,000
2003	$235,143	50.0%	$117,595	$352,738	$4,000
2004	$356,738	8.6%	$30,679	$387,418	$4,000
2005	$391,418	3.3%	$12,917	$404,335	$4,000
2006	$408,335	9.5%	$38,792	$447,126	$4,000
2008	$451,126	9.8%	$44,255	$495,382	$4,000
2008	$499,382	-40.5%	($202,449)	$296,932	$4,000
2009	$300,932	43.9%	$132,079	$433,012	$4,000
2010	$437,012	16.9%	$73,899	$510,910	$4,000
2011	$514,910	-1.8%	($9,268)	$505,642	$4,000
2012	$509,642	15.8%	$80,625	$590,267	
	Total	**394.7%**		**Investment**	**$124,000**
	Years	**31**			
	Simple Rate	**12.7%**	**Real Rate**	**8.5%**	

Appendix A (Chapter 12) con't
Calculating NASDAQ Simple Rate of 12.7%

Year	Starting Payment	Simple Rate of Return	Interest	Total	Next Payment
1982	$4,000	12.7%	$509	$4,509	$4,000
1983	$8,509	12.7%	$1,083	$9,593	$4,000
1984	$13,593	12.7%	$1,731	$15,323	$4,000
1985	$19,323	12.7%	$2,460	$21,783	$4,000
1986	$25,783	12.7%	$3,283	$29,066	$4,000
1987	$33,066	12.7%	$4,210	$37,275	$4,000
1988	$41,275	12.7%	$5,255	$46,530	$4,000
1989	$50,530	12.7%	$6,433	$56,963	$4,000
1990	$60,963	12.7%	$7,761	$68,725	$4,000
1991	$72,725	12.7%	$9,259	$81,984	$4,000
1992	$85,984	12.7%	$10,947	$96,931	$4,000
1993	$100,931	12.7%	$12,850	$113,780	$4,000
1994	$117,780	12.7%	$14,995	$132,775	$4,000
1995	$136,775	12.7%	$17,413	$154,189	$4,000
1996	$158,189	12.7%	$20,139	$178,328	$4,000
1997	$182,328	12.7%	$23,213	$205,541	$4,000
1998	$209,541	12.7%	$26,677	$236,218	$4,000
1999	$240,218	12.7%	$30,583	$270,801	$4,000
2000	$274,801	12.7%	$34,986	$309,786	$4,000
2001	$313,786	12.7%	$39,949	$353,735	$4,000
2002	$357,735	12.7%	$45,544	$403,280	$4,000
2003	$407,280	12.7%	$51,852	$459,132	$4,000
2004	$463,132	12.7%	$58,963	$522,094	$4,000
2005	$526,094	12.7%	$66,979	$593,073	$4,000
2006	$597,073	12.7%	$76,015	$673,088	$4,000
2008	$677,088	12.7%	$86,202	$763,290	$4,000
2008	$767,290	12.7%	$97,686	$864,976	$4,000
2009	$868,976	12.7%	$110,632	$979,608	$4,000
2010	$983,608	12.7%	$125,226	$1,108,834	$4,000
2011	$1,112,834	12.7%	$141,678	$1,254,512	$4,000
2012	$1,258,512	12.7%	$160,225	$1,418,737	
Total		**12.7%**		**Investment**	**$124,000**

Appendix B (Chapter 14)
Investing $4,000 Per Year in a
Taxable Account Earning 8%

Year	Initial Savings	Rate Earned	Earnings	Total	Tax Rate	Tax Owed	Remaining	New Savings
1	$4,000	8.00%	$320	$4,320	25%	$80	$4,240	$4,000
2	$8,240	8.00%	$659	$8,899	25%	$165	$8,734	$4,000
3	$12,734	8.00%	$1,019	$13,753	25%	$255	$13,498	$4,000
4	$17,498	8.00%	$1,400	$18,898	25%	$350	$18,548	$4,000
5	$22,548	8.00%	$1,804	$24,352	25%	$451	$23,901	$4,000
6	$27,901	8.00%	$2,232	$30,133	25%	$558	$29,575	$4,000
7	$33,575	8.00%	$2,686	$36,261	25%	$672	$35,590	$4,000
8	$39,590	8.00%	$3,167	$42,757	25%	$792	$41,965	$4,000
9	$45,965	8.00%	$3,677	$49,642	25%	$919	$48,723	$4,000
10	$52,723	8.00%	$4,218	$56,941	25%	$1,054	$55,887	$4,000
11	$59,887	8.00%	$4,791	$64,677	25%	$1,198	$63,480	$4,000
12	$67,480	8.00%	$5,398	$72,878	25%	$1,350	$71,529	$4,000
13	$75,529	8.00%	$6,042	$81,571	25%	$1,511	$80,060	$4,000
14	$84,060	8.00%	$6,725	$90,785	25%	$1,681	$89,104	$4,000
15	$93,104	8.00%	$7,448	$100,552	25%	$1,862	$98,690	$4,000
16	$102,690	8.00%	$8,215	$110,905	25%	$2,054	$108,852	$4,000
17	$112,852	8.00%	$9,028	$121,880	25%	$2,257	$119,623	$4,000
18	$123,623	8.00%	$9,890	$133,512	25%	$2,472	$131,040	$4,000
19	$135,040	8.00%	$10,803	$145,843	25%	$2,701	$143,142	$4,000
20	$147,142	8.00%	$11,771	$158,914	25%	$2,943	$155,971	$4,000
21	$159,971	8.00%	$12,798	$172,769	25%	$3,199	$169,569	$4,000
22	$173,569	8.00%	$13,886	$187,455	25%	$3,471	$183,983	$4,000
23	$187,983	8.00%	$15,039	$203,022	25%	$3,760	$199,262	$4,000
24	$203,262	8.00%	$16,261	$219,523	25%	$4,065	$215,458	$4,000
25	$219,458	8.00%	$17,557	$237,015	25%	$4,389	$232,626	$4,000
26	$236,626	8.00%	$18,930	$255,556	25%	$4,733	$250,823	$4,000
27	$254,823	8.00%	$20,386	$275,209	25%	$5,096	$270,112	$4,000
28	$274,112	8.00%	$21,929	$296,041	25%	$5,482	$290,559	$4,000
29	$294,559	8.00%	$23,565	$318,124	25%	$5,891	$312,233	$4,000
30	$316,233	8.00%	$25,299	$341,531	25%	$6,325	**$335,207**	

Appendix B (Chapter 14) con't
Investing $4,000 per Year in a Tax-deferred
Account Earning the Same 8%

Year	Initial Savings	Rate Earned	Earnings	Total	New Savings	Tax Rate	Tax Savings
1	$4,000	8.00%	$320	$4,320	$4,000	25%	$1,000
2	$8,320	8.00%	$666	$8,986	$4,000	25%	$1,000
3	$12,986	8.00%	$1,039	$14,024	$4,000	25%	$1,000
4	$18,024	8.00%	$1,442	$19,466	$4,000	25%	$1,000
5	$23,466	8.00%	$1,877	$25,344	$4,000	25%	$1,000
6	$29,344	8.00%	$2,347	$31,691	$4,000	25%	$1,000
7	$35,691	8.00%	$2,855	$38,547	$4,000	25%	$1,000
8	$42,547	8.00%	$3,404	$45,950	$4,000	25%	$1,000
9	$49,950	8.00%	$3,996	$53,946	$4,000	25%	$1,000
10	$57,946	8.00%	$4,636	$62,582	$4,000	25%	$1,000
11	$66,582	8.00%	$5,327	$71,909	$4,000	25%	$1,000
12	$75,909	8.00%	$6,073	$81,981	$4,000	25%	$1,000
13	$85,981	8.00%	$6,878	$92,860	$4,000	25%	$1,000
14	$96,860	8.00%	$7,749	$104,608	$4,000	25%	$1,000
15	$108,608	8.00%	$8,689	$117,297	$4,000	25%	$1,000
16	$121,297	8.00%	$9,704	$131,001	$4,000	25%	$1,000
17	$135,001	8.00%	$10,800	$145,801	$4,000	25%	$1,000
18	$149,801	8.00%	$11,984	$161,785	$4,000	25%	$1,000
19	$165,785	8.00%	$13,263	$179,048	$4,000	25%	$1,000
20	$183,048	8.00%	$14,644	$197,692	$4,000	25%	$1,000
21	$201,692	8.00%	$16,135	$217,827	$4,000	25%	$1,000
22	$221,827	8.00%	$17,746	$239,573	$4,000	25%	$1,000
23	$243,573	8.00%	$19,486	$263,059	$4,000	25%	$1,000
24	$267,059	8.00%	$21,365	$288,424	$4,000	25%	$1,000
25	$292,424	8.00%	$23,394	$315,818	$4,000	25%	$1,000
26	$319,818	8.00%	$25,585	$345,403	$4,000	25%	$1,000
27	$349,403	8.00%	$27,952	$377,355	$4,000	25%	$1,000
28	$381,355	8.00%	$30,508	$411,864	$4,000	25%	$1,000
29	$415,864	8.00%	$33,269	$449,133	$4,000	25%	$1,000
30	$453,133	8.00%	$36,251	**$489,383**	$4,000	25%	$1,000
			After 25% Tax	**$367,038**			$30,000
			Savings Acct	**$335,207**			
			Total	**$31,831**			
			After 15% Tax	**$415,976**			
			Savings Acct	**$335,207**			
			Total	**$80,769**			

Appendix B (Chapter 14)
Investing the $1,000 Tax Savings
in a Roth IRA for 30 Years

Year	Tax Savings	Initial Savings	Rate Earned	Earnings	Total
1	$1,000	$1,000	8.00%	$80	$1,080
2	$1,000	$2,080	8.00%	$166	$2,246
3	$1,000	$3,246	8.00%	$260	$3,506
4	$1,000	$4,506	8.00%	$360	$4,867
5	$1,000	$5,867	8.00%	$469	$6,336
6	$1,000	$7,336	8.00%	$587	$7,923
7	$1,000	$8,923	8.00%	$714	$9,637
8	$1,000	$10,637	8.00%	$851	$11,488
9	$1,000	$12,488	8.00%	$999	$13,487
10	$1,000	$14,487	8.00%	$1,159	$15,645
11	$1,000	$16,645	8.00%	$1,332	$17,977
12	$1,000	$18,977	8.00%	$1,518	$20,495
13	$1,000	$21,495	8.00%	$1,720	$23,215
14	$1,000	$24,215	8.00%	$1,937	$26,152
15	$1,000	$27,152	8.00%	$2,172	$29,324
16	$1,000	$30,324	8.00%	$2,426	$32,750
17	$1,000	$33,750	8.00%	$2,700	$36,450
18	$1,000	$37,450	8.00%	$2,996	$40,446
19	$1,000	$41,446	8.00%	$3,316	$44,762
20	$1,000	$45,762	8.00%	$3,661	$49,423
21	$1,000	$50,423	8.00%	$4,034	$54,457
22	$1,000	$55,457	8.00%	$4,437	$59,893
23	$1,000	$60,893	8.00%	$4,871	$65,765
24	$1,000	$66,765	8.00%	$5,341	$72,106
25	$1,000	$73,106	8.00%	$5,848	$78,954
26	$1,000	$79,954	8.00%	$6,396	$86,351
27	$1,000	$87,351	8.00%	$6,988	$94,339
28	$1,000	$95,339	8.00%	$7,627	$102,966
29	$1,000	$103,966	8.00%	$8,317	$112,283
30	$30,000	$113,283	8.00%	$9,063	**$122,346**

Appendix C (Chapter 15)

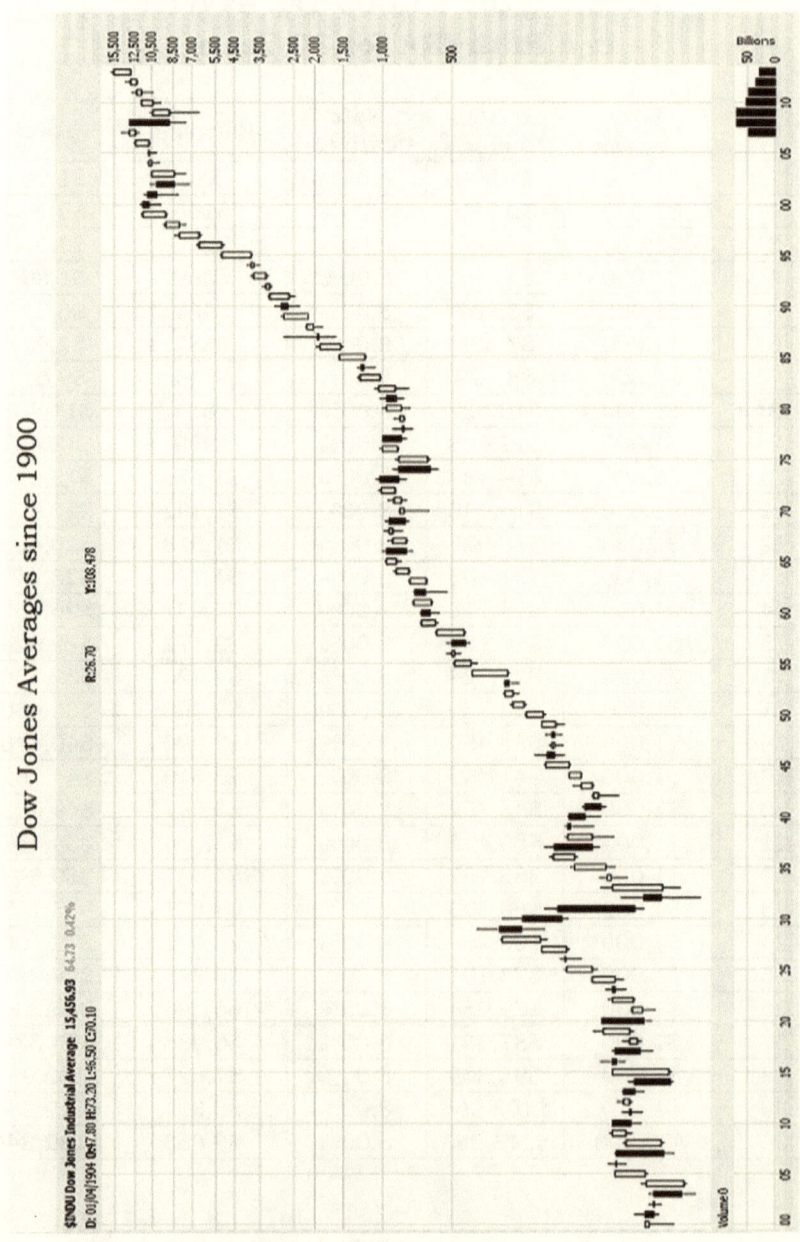

Chart courtesy of TD Ameritrade.

Appendix D (Chapter 18)—Russell Small Cap

Year	Starting Amount	Rate of Return	Interest Earned	Ending Balance
1980	$100	25.4%	$25	$125
1981	$125	14.9%	$19	$144
1982	$144	28.5%	$41	$185
1983	$185	38.6%	$71	$257
1984	$257	2.3%	$6	$262
1985	$262	31.0%	$81	$344
1986	$344	7.4%	$25	$369
1987	$369	**-7.1%**	($26)	$343
1988	$343	29.5%	$101	$444
1989	$444	12.4%	$55	$499
1990	$499	**-21.8%**	($109)	$391
1991	$391	41.7%	$163	$553
1992	$553	29.1%	$161	$715
1993	$715	23.8%	$170	$885
1994	$885	**-1.5%**	($14)	$871
1995	$871	25.8%	$224	$1,095
1996	$1,095	21.4%	$234	$1,329
1997	$1,329	31.8%	$422	$1,752
1998	$1,752	**-6.5%**	($113)	$1,639
1999	$1,639	**-1.5%**	($24)	$1,614
2000	$1,614	22.8%	$369	$1,983
2001	$1,983	14.0%	$278	$2,261
2002	$2,261	**-11.4%**	($258)	$2,003
2003	$2,003	46.0%	$922	$2,924
2004	$2,924	22.3%	$651	$3,575
2005	$3,575	4.7%	$168	$3,743
2006	$3,743	23.5%	$879	$4,622
2007	$4,622	**-9.8%**	($452)	$4,170
2008	$4,170	**-28.9%**	($1,206)	$2,964
2009	$2,964	20.6%	$610	$3,574
2010	$3,574	24.5%	$876	$4,450
2011	$4,450	**-5.5%**	($245)	$4,205
2012	$4,205	14.4%	$603	$4,809
Real Ret	**12.45%**			

Appendix E (Chapter 22)
Saving $400/Month/30 Years/8%

Number Of Contributions	Total Contribution	Monthly Return 8% ÷ 12	Interest Earned	Month End Total	Next Month Contribution
1	$400	0.67%	$2.7	$403	$400
2	$803	0.67%	$5.4	$808	$400
3	$1,208	0.67%	$8.1	$1,216	$400
4	$1,616	0.67%	$10.8	$1,627	$400
5	$2,027	0.67%	$13.6	$2,041	$400
6	$2,441	0.67%	$16.4	$2,457	$400
7	$2,857	0.67%	$19.1	$2,876	$400
8	$3,276	0.67%	$21.9	$3,298	$400
9	$3,698	0.67%	$24.8	$3,723	$400
10	$4,123	0.67%	$27.6	$4,150	$400
11	$4,550	0.67%	$30.5	$4,581	$400
12	$4,981	0.67%	$33.4	$5,014	$400
13	$5,414	0.67%	$36.3	$5,451	$400
14	$5,851	0.67%	$39.2	$5,890	$400
15	$6,290	0.67%	$42.1	$6,332	$400
16	$6,732	0.67%	$45.1	$6,777	$400
17	$7,177	0.67%	$48.1	$7,225	$400
18	$7,625	0.67%	$51.1	$7,676	$400
19	$8,076	0.67%	$54.1	$8,130	$400
20	$8,530	0.67%	$57.2	$8,587	$400
21	$8,987	0.67%	$60.2	$9,048	$400
22	$9,448	0.67%	$63.3	$9,511	$400
23	$9,911	0.67%	$66.4	$9,977	$400
24	$10,377	0.67%	$69.5	$10,447	$400
25	$10,847	0.67%	$72.7	$10,920	$400
26	$11,320	0.67%	$75.8	$11,395	$400
27	$11,795	0.67%	$79.0	$11,874	$400
28	$12,274	0.67%	$82.2	$12,357	$400
29	$12,757	0.67%	$85.5	$12,842	$400
30	$13,242	0.67%	$88.7	$13,331	$400
31	$13,731	0.67%	$92.0	$13,823	$400
32	$14,223	0.67%	$95.3	$14,318	$400
33	$14,718	0.67%	$98.6	$14,817	$400
34	$15,217	0.67%	$102.0	$15,319	$400
35	$15,719	0.67%	$105.3	$15,824	$400
36	$16,224	0.67%	$108.7	$16,333	$400

Number Of Contributions	Total Contribution	Monthly Return 8% ÷ 12	Interest Earned	Month End Total	Next Month Contribution
37	$16,733	0.67%	$112.1	$16,845	$400
38	$17,245	0.67%	$115.5	$17,360	$400
39	$17,760	0.67%	$119.0	$17,879	$400
40	$18,279	0.67%	$122.5	$18,402	$400
41	$18,802	0.67%	$126.0	$18,928	$400
42	$19,328	0.67%	$129.5	$19,457	$400
43	$19,857	0.67%	$133.0	$19,990	$400
44	$20,390	0.67%	$136.6	$20,527	$400
45	$20,927	0.67%	$140.2	$21,067	$400
46	$21,467	0.67%	$143.8	$21,611	$400
47	$22,011	0.67%	$147.5	$22,158	$400
48	$22,558	0.67%	$151.1	$22,710	$400
49	$23,110	0.67%	$154.8	$23,264	$400
50	$23,664	0.67%	$158.6	$23,823	$400
51	$24,223	0.67%	$162.3	$24,385	$400
52	$24,785	0.67%	$166.1	$24,951	$400
53	$25,351	0.67%	$169.9	$25,521	$400
54	$25,921	0.67%	$173.7	$26,095	$400
55	$26,495	0.67%	$177.5	$26,672	$400
56	$27,072	0.67%	$181.4	$27,254	$400
57	$27,654	0.67%	$185.3	$27,839	$400
58	$28,239	0.67%	$189.2	$28,428	$400
59	$28,828	0.67%	$193.1	$29,021	$400
60	$29,421	0.67%	$197.1	$29,619	$400
61	$30,019	0.67%	$201.1	$30,220	$400
62	$30,620	0.67%	$205.2	$30,825	$400
63	$31,225	0.67%	$209.2	$31,434	$400
64	$31,834	0.67%	$213.3	$32,047	$400
65	$32,447	0.67%	$217.4	$32,665	$400
66	$33,065	0.67%	$221.5	$33,286	$400
67	$33,686	0.67%	$225.7	$33,912	$400
68	$34,312	0.67%	$229.9	$34,542	$400
69	$34,942	0.67%	$234.1	$35,176	$400
70	$35,576	0.67%	$238.4	$35,814	$400
71	$36,214	0.67%	$242.6	$36,457	$400
72	$36,857	0.67%	$246.9	$37,104	$400
73	$37,504	0.67%	$251.3	$37,755	$400
74	$38,155	0.67%	$255.6	$38,411	$400
75	$38,811	0.67%	$260.0	$39,071	$400
76	$39,471	0.67%	$264.5	$39,735	$400

Number Of Contributions	Total Contribution	Monthly Return 8% ÷ 12	Interest Earned	Month End Total	Next Month Contribution
77	$40,135	0.67%	$268.9	$40,404	$400
78	$40,804	0.67%	$273.4	$41,078	$400
79	$41,478	0.67%	$277.9	$41,755	$400
80	$42,155	0.67%	$282.4	$42,438	$400
81	$42,838	0.67%	$287.0	$43,125	$400
82	$43,525	0.67%	$291.6	$43,817	$400
83	$44,217	0.67%	$296.3	$44,513	$400
84	$44,913	0.67%	$300.9	$45,214	$400
85	$45,614	0.67%	$305.6	$45,919	$400
86	$46,319	0.67%	$310.3	$46,630	$400
87	$47,030	0.67%	$315.1	$47,345	$400
88	$47,745	0.67%	$319.9	$48,065	$400
89	$48,465	0.67%	$324.7	$48,789	$400
90	$49,189	0.67%	$329.6	$49,519	$400
91	$49,919	0.67%	$334.5	$50,253	$400
92	$50,653	0.67%	$339.4	$50,993	$400
93	$51,393	0.67%	$344.3	$51,737	$400
94	$52,137	0.67%	$349.3	$52,486	$400
95	$52,886	0.67%	$354.3	$53,241	$400
96	$53,641	0.67%	$359.4	$54,000	$400
97	$54,400	0.67%	$364.5	$54,765	$400
98	$55,165	0.67%	$369.6	$55,534	$400
99	$55,934	0.67%	$374.8	$56,309	$400
100	$56,709	0.67%	$380.0	$57,089	$400
101	$57,489	0.67%	$385.2	$57,874	$400
102	$58,274	0.67%	$390.4	$58,665	$400
103	$59,065	0.67%	$395.7	$59,460	$400
104	$59,860	0.67%	$401.1	$60,261	$400
105	$60,661	0.67%	$406.4	$61,068	$400
106	$61,468	0.67%	$411.8	$61,880	$400
107	$62,280	0.67%	$417.3	$62,697	$400
108	$63,097	0.67%	$422.7	$63,520	$400
109	$63,920	0.67%	$428.3	$64,348	$400
110	$64,748	0.67%	$433.8	$65,182	$400
111	$65,582	0.67%	$439.4	$66,021	$400
112	$66,421	0.67%	$445.0	$66,866	$400
113	$67,266	0.67%	$450.7	$67,717	$400
114	$68,117	0.67%	$456.4	$68,573	$400
115	$68,973	0.67%	$462.1	$69,435	$400
116	$69,835	0.67%	$467.9	$70,303	$400

Number Of Contributions	Total Contribution	Monthly Return 8% ÷ 12	Interest Earned	Month End Total	Next Month Contribution
117	$70,703	0.67%	$473.7	$71,177	$400
118	$71,577	0.67%	$479.6	$72,056	$400
119	$72,456	0.67%	$485.5	$72,942	$400
120	$73,342	0.67%	$491.4	$73,833	$400
121	$74,233	0.67%	$497.4	$74,731	$400
122	$75,131	0.67%	$503.4	$75,634	$400
123	$76,034	0.67%	$509.4	$76,543	$400
124	$76,943	0.67%	$515.5	$77,459	$400
125	$77,859	0.67%	$521.7	$78,381	$400
126	$78,781	0.67%	$527.8	$79,308	$400
127	$79,708	0.67%	$534.0	$80,243	$400
128	$80,643	0.67%	$540.3	$81,183	$400
129	$81,583	0.67%	$546.6	$82,129	$400
130	$82,529	0.67%	$552.9	$83,082	$400
131	$83,482	0.67%	$559.3	$84,042	$400
132	$84,442	0.67%	$565.8	$85,007	$400
133	$85,407	0.67%	$572.2	$85,980	$400
134	$86,380	0.67%	$578.7	$86,958	$400
135	$87,358	0.67%	$585.3	$87,944	$400
136	$88,344	0.67%	$591.9	$88,936	$400
137	$89,336	0.67%	$598.5	$89,934	$400
138	$90,334	0.67%	$605.2	$90,939	$400
139	$91,339	0.67%	$612.0	$91,951	$400
140	$92,351	0.67%	$618.8	$92,970	$400
141	$93,370	0.67%	$625.6	$93,996	$400
142	$94,396	0.67%	$632.5	$95,028	$400
143	$95,428	0.67%	$639.4	$96,068	$400
144	$96,468	0.67%	$646.3	$97,114	$400
145	$97,514	0.67%	$653.3	$98,167	$400
146	$98,567	0.67%	$660.4	$99,228	$400
147	$99,628	0.67%	$667.5	$100,295	$400
148	$100,695	0.67%	$674.7	$101,370	$400
149	$101,770	0.67%	$681.9	$102,452	$400
150	$102,852	0.67%	$689.1	$103,541	$400
151	$103,941	0.67%	$696.4	$104,637	$400
152	$105,037	0.67%	$703.7	$105,741	$400
153	$106,141	0.67%	$711.1	$106,852	$400
154	$107,252	0.67%	$718.6	$107,971	$400
155	$108,371	0.67%	$726.1	$109,097	$400
156	$109,497	0.67%	$733.6	$110,230	$400

Number Of Contributions	Total Contribution	Monthly Return 8% ÷ 12	Interest Earned	Month End Total	Next Month Contribution
157	$110,630	0.67%	$741.2	$111,372	$400
158	$111,772	0.67%	$748.9	$112,520	$400
159	$112,920	0.67%	$756.6	$113,677	$400
160	$114,077	0.67%	$764.3	$114,841	$400
161	$115,241	0.67%	$772.1	$116,013	$400
162	$116,413	0.67%	$780.0	$117,193	$400
163	$117,593	0.67%	$787.9	$118,381	$400
164	$118,781	0.67%	$795.8	$119,577	$400
165	$119,977	0.67%	$803.8	$120,781	$400
166	$121,181	0.67%	$811.9	$121,993	$400
167	$122,393	0.67%	$820.0	$123,213	$400
168	$123,613	0.67%	$828.2	$124,441	$400
169	$124,841	0.67%	$836.4	$125,678	$400
170	$126,078	0.67%	$844.7	$126,922	$400
171	$127,322	0.67%	$853.1	$128,175	$400
172	$128,575	0.67%	$861.5	$129,437	$400
173	$129,837	0.67%	$869.9	$130,707	$400
174	$131,107	0.67%	$878.4	$131,985	$400
175	$132,385	0.67%	$887.0	$133,272	$400
176	$133,672	0.67%	$895.6	$134,568	$400
177	$134,968	0.67%	$904.3	$135,872	$400
178	$136,272	0.67%	$913.0	$137,185	$400
179	$137,585	0.67%	$921.8	$138,507	$400
180	$138,907	0.67%	$930.7	$139,838	$400
181	$140,238	0.67%	$939.6	$141,177	$400
182	$141,577	0.67%	$948.6	$142,526	$400
183	$142,926	0.67%	$957.6	$143,883	$400
184	$144,283	0.67%	$966.7	$145,250	$400
185	$145,650	0.67%	$975.9	$146,626	$400
186	$147,026	0.67%	$985.1	$148,011	$400
187	$148,411	0.67%	$994.4	$149,405	$400
188	$149,805	0.67%	$1,003.7	$150,809	$400
189	$151,209	0.67%	$1,013.1	$152,222	$400
190	$152,622	0.67%	$1,022.6	$153,645	$400
191	$154,045	0.67%	$1,032.1	$155,077	$400
192	$155,477	0.67%	$1,041.7	$156,518	$400
193	$156,918	0.67%	$1,051.4	$157,970	$400
194	$158,370	0.67%	$1,061.1	$159,431	$400
195	$159,831	0.67%	$1,070.9	$160,902	$400
196	$161,302	0.67%	$1,080.7	$162,382	$400

Number Of Contributions	Total Contribution	Monthly Return 8% ÷ 12	Interest Earned	Month End Total	Next Month Contribution
197	$162,782	0.67%	$1,090.6	$163,873	$400
198	$164,273	0.67%	$1,100.6	$165,374	$400
199	$165,774	0.67%	$1,110.7	$166,884	$400
200	$167,284	0.67%	$1,120.8	$168,405	$400
201	$168,805	0.67%	$1,131.0	$169,936	$400
202	$170,336	0.67%	$1,141.3	$171,477	$400
203	$171,877	0.67%	$1,151.6	$173,029	$400
204	$173,429	0.67%	$1,162.0	$174,591	$400
205	$174,991	0.67%	$1,172.4	$176,163	$400
206	$176,563	0.67%	$1,183.0	$177,746	$400
207	$178,146	0.67%	$1,193.6	$179,340	$400
208	$179,740	0.67%	$1,204.3	$180,944	$400
209	$181,344	0.67%	$1,215.0	$182,559	$400
210	$182,959	0.67%	$1,225.8	$184,185	$400
211	$184,585	0.67%	$1,236.7	$185,822	$400
212	$186,222	0.67%	$1,247.7	$187,470	$400
213	$187,870	0.67%	$1,258.7	$189,128	$400
214	$189,528	0.67%	$1,269.8	$190,798	$400
215	$191,198	0.67%	$1,281.0	$192,479	$400
216	$192,879	0.67%	$1,292.3	$194,171	$400
217	$194,571	0.67%	$1,303.6	$195,875	$400
218	$196,275	0.67%	$1,315.0	$197,590	$400
219	$197,990	0.67%	$1,326.5	$199,317	$400
220	$199,717	0.67%	$1,338.1	$201,055	$400
221	$201,455	0.67%	$1,349.7	$202,804	$400
222	$203,204	0.67%	$1,361.5	$204,566	$400
223	$204,966	0.67%	$1,373.3	$206,339	$400
224	$206,739	0.67%	$1,385.2	$208,124	$400
225	$208,524	0.67%	$1,397.1	$209,921	$400
226	$210,321	0.67%	$1,409.2	$211,731	$400
227	$212,131	0.67%	$1,421.3	$213,552	$400
228	$213,952	0.67%	$1,433.5	$215,385	$400
229	$215,785	0.67%	$1,445.8	$217,231	$400
230	$217,631	0.67%	$1,458.1	$219,089	$400
231	$219,489	0.67%	$1,470.6	$220,960	$400
232	$221,360	0.67%	$1,483.1	$222,843	$400
233	$223,243	0.67%	$1,495.7	$224,739	$400
234	$225,139	0.67%	$1,508.4	$226,647	$400
235	$227,047	0.67%	$1,521.2	$228,568	$400
236	$228,968	0.67%	$1,534.1	$230,502	$400

Number Of Contributions	Total Contribution	Monthly Return 8% ÷ 12	Interest Earned	Month End Total	Next Month Contribution
237	$230,902	0.67%	$1,547.0	$232,449	$400
238	$232,849	0.67%	$1,560.1	$234,410	$400
239	$234,810	0.67%	$1,573.2	$236,383	$400
240	$236,783	0.67%	$1,586.4	$238,369	$400
241	$238,769	0.67%	$1,599.8	$240,369	$400
242	$240,769	0.67%	$1,613.2	$242,382	$400
243	$242,782	0.67%	$1,626.6	$244,409	$400
244	$244,809	0.67%	$1,640.2	$246,449	$400
245	$246,849	0.67%	$1,653.9	$248,503	$400
246	$248,903	0.67%	$1,667.6	$250,571	$400
247	$250,971	0.67%	$1,681.5	$252,652	$400
248	$253,052	0.67%	$1,695.4	$254,747	$400
249	$255,147	0.67%	$1,709.5	$256,857	$400
250	$257,257	0.67%	$1,723.6	$258,981	$400
251	$259,381	0.67%	$1,737.8	$261,118	$400
252	$261,518	0.67%	$1,752.2	$263,271	$400
253	$263,671	0.67%	$1,766.6	$265,437	$400
254	$265,837	0.67%	$1,781.1	$267,618	$400
255	$268,018	0.67%	$1,795.7	$269,814	$400
256	$270,214	0.67%	$1,810.4	$272,024	$400
257	$272,424	0.67%	$1,825.2	$274,250	$400
258	$274,650	0.67%	$1,840.2	$276,490	$400
259	$276,890	0.67%	$1,855.2	$278,745	$400
260	$279,145	0.67%	$1,870.3	$281,015	$400
261	$281,415	0.67%	$1,885.5	$283,301	$400
262	$283,701	0.67%	$1,900.8	$285,602	$400
263	$286,002	0.67%	$1,916.2	$287,918	$400
264	$288,318	0.67%	$1,931.7	$290,250	$400
265	$290,650	0.67%	$1,947.4	$292,597	$400
266	$292,997	0.67%	$1,963.1	$294,960	$400
267	$295,360	0.67%	$1,978.9	$297,339	$400
268	$297,739	0.67%	$1,994.9	$299,734	$400
269	$300,134	0.67%	$2,010.9	$302,145	$400
270	$302,545	0.67%	$2,027.0	$304,572	$400
271	$304,972	0.67%	$2,043.3	$307,015	$400
272	$307,415	0.67%	$2,059.7	$309,475	$400
273	$309,875	0.67%	$2,076.2	$311,951	$400
274	$312,351	0.67%	$2,092.8	$314,444	$400
275	$314,844	0.67%	$2,109.5	$316,953	$400
276	$317,353	0.67%	$2,126.3	$319,479	$400

Number Of Contributions	Total Contribution	Monthly Return 8% ÷ 12	Interest Earned	Month End Total	Next Month Contribution
277	$319,879	0.67%	$2,143.2	$322,022	$400
278	$322,422	0.67%	$2,160.2	$324,583	$400
279	$324,983	0.67%	$2,177.4	$327,160	$400
280	$327,560	0.67%	$2,194.7	$329,755	$400
281	$330,155	0.67%	$2,212.0	$332,367	$400
282	$332,767	0.67%	$2,229.5	$334,996	$400
283	$335,396	0.67%	$2,247.2	$337,643	$400
284	$338,043	0.67%	$2,264.9	$340,308	$400
285	$340,708	0.67%	$2,282.7	$342,991	$400
286	$343,391	0.67%	$2,300.7	$345,692	$400
287	$346,092	0.67%	$2,318.8	$348,411	$400
288	$348,811	0.67%	$2,337.0	$351,148	$400
289	$351,548	0.67%	$2,355.4	$353,903	$400
290	$354,303	0.67%	$2,373.8	$356,677	$400
291	$357,077	0.67%	$2,392.4	$359,469	$400
292	$359,869	0.67%	$2,411.1	$362,280	$400
293	$362,680	0.67%	$2,430.0	$365,110	$400
294	$365,510	0.67%	$2,448.9	$367,959	$400
295	$368,359	0.67%	$2,468.0	$370,827	$400
296	$371,227	0.67%	$2,487.2	$373,715	$400
297	$374,115	0.67%	$2,506.6	$376,621	$400
298	$377,021	0.67%	$2,526.0	$379,547	$400
299	$379,947	0.67%	$2,545.6	$382,493	$400
300	$382,893	0.67%	$2,565.4	$385,458	$400
301	$385,858	0.67%	$2,585.2	$388,443	$400
302	$388,843	0.67%	$2,605.3	$391,449	$400
303	$391,849	0.67%	$2,625.4	$394,474	$400
304	$394,874	0.67%	$2,645.7	$397,520	$400
305	$397,920	0.67%	$2,666.1	$400,586	$400
306	$400,986	0.67%	$2,686.6	$403,672	$400
307	$404,072	0.67%	$2,707.3	$406,780	$400
308	$407,180	0.67%	$2,728.1	$409,908	$400
309	$410,308	0.67%	$2,749.1	$413,057	$400
310	$413,457	0.67%	$2,770.2	$416,227	$400
311	$416,627	0.67%	$2,791.4	$419,418	$400
312	$419,818	0.67%	$2,812.8	$422,631	$400
313	$423,031	0.67%	$2,834.3	$425,865	$400
314	$426,265	0.67%	$2,856.0	$429,121	$400
315	$429,521	0.67%	$2,877.8	$432,399	$400
316	$432,799	0.67%	$2,899.8	$435,699	$400

Number Of Contributions	Total Contribution	Monthly Return 8% ÷ 12	Interest Earned	Month End Total	Next Month Contribution
317	$436,099	0.67%	$2,921.9	$439,021	$400
318	$439,421	0.67%	$2,944.1	$442,365	$400
319	$442,765	0.67%	$2,966.5	$445,731	$400
320	$446,131	0.67%	$2,989.1	$449,121	$400
321	$449,521	0.67%	$3,011.8	$452,532	$400
322	$452,932	0.67%	$3,034.6	$455,967	$400
323	$456,367	0.67%	$3,057.7	$459,425	$400
324	$459,825	0.67%	$3,080.8	$462,905	$400
325	$463,305	0.67%	$3,104.1	$466,410	$400
326	$466,810	0.67%	$3,127.6	$469,937	$400
327	$470,337	0.67%	$3,151.3	$473,489	$400
328	$473,889	0.67%	$3,175.1	$477,064	$400
329	$477,464	0.67%	$3,199.0	$480,663	$400
330	$481,063	0.67%	$3,223.1	$484,286	$400
331	$484,686	0.67%	$3,247.4	$487,933	$400
332	$488,333	0.67%	$3,271.8	$491,605	$400
333	$492,005	0.67%	$3,296.4	$495,301	$400
334	$495,701	0.67%	$3,321.2	$499,023	$400
335	$499,423	0.67%	$3,346.1	$502,769	$400
336	$503,169	0.67%	$3,371.2	$506,540	$400
337	$506,940	0.67%	$3,396.5	$510,336	$400
338	$510,736	0.67%	$3,421.9	$514,158	$400
339	$514,558	0.67%	$3,447.5	$518,006	$400
340	$518,406	0.67%	$3,473.3	$521,879	$400
341	$522,279	0.67%	$3,499.3	$525,778	$400
342	$526,178	0.67%	$3,525.4	$529,704	$400
343	$530,104	0.67%	$3,551.7	$533,656	$400
344	$534,056	0.67%	$3,578.2	$537,634	$400
345	$538,034	0.67%	$3,604.8	$541,639	$400
346	$542,039	0.67%	$3,631.7	$545,670	$400
347	$546,070	0.67%	$3,658.7	$549,729	$400
348	$550,129	0.67%	$3,685.9	$553,815	$400
349	$554,215	0.67%	$3,713.2	$557,928	$400
350	$558,328	0.67%	$3,740.8	$562,069	$400
351	$562,469	0.67%	$3,768.5	$566,237	$400
352	$566,637	0.67%	$3,796.5	$570,434	$400
353	$570,834	0.67%	$3,824.6	$574,658	$400
354	$575,058	0.67%	$3,852.9	$578,911	$400
355	$579,311	0.67%	$3,881.4	$583,193	$400
356	$583,593	0.67%	$3,910.1	$587,503	$400

Number Of Contributions	Total Contribution	Monthly Return 8% ÷ 12	Interest Earned	Month End Total	Next Month Contribution
357	$587,903	0.67%	$3,938.9	$591,842	$400
358	$592,242	0.67%	$3,968.0	$596,210	$400
359	$596,610	0.67%	$3,997.3	$600,607	$400
360	$601,007	0.67%	$4,026.7	**$605,034**	

Appendix F (Chapter 22)
Saving $400/Month/30 Years/12%

Number Of Contributions	Monthly Contribution	Monthly Return 12% ÷ 12	Interest Earned	Month End Total	Next Month Contribution
1	$400	1.00%	$4.0	$404	$400
2	$804	1.00%	$8.0	$812	$400
3	$1,212	1.00%	$12.1	$1,224	$400
4	$1,624	1.00%	$16.2	$1,640	$400
5	$2,040	1.00%	$20.4	$2,061	$400
6	$2,461	1.00%	$24.6	$2,485	$400
7	$2,885	1.00%	$28.9	$2,914	$400
8	$3,314	1.00%	$33.1	$3,347	$400
9	$3,747	1.00%	$37.5	$3,785	$400
10	$4,185	1.00%	$41.8	$4,227	$400
11	$4,627	1.00%	$46.3	$4,673	$400
12	$5,073	1.00%	$50.7	$5,124	$400
13	$5,524	1.00%	$55.2	$5,579	$400
14	$5,979	1.00%	$59.8	$6,039	$400
15	$6,439	1.00%	$64.4	$6,503	$400
16	$6,903	1.00%	$69.0	$6,972	$400
17	$7,372	1.00%	$73.7	$7,446	$400
18	$7,846	1.00%	$78.5	$7,924	$400
19	$8,324	1.00%	$83.2	$8,408	$400
20	$8,808	1.00%	$88.1	$8,896	$400
21	$9,296	1.00%	$93.0	$9,389	$400
22	$9,789	1.00%	$97.9	$9,887	$400
23	$10,287	1.00%	$102.9	$10,389	$400
24	$10,789	1.00%	$107.9	$10,897	$400
25	$11,297	1.00%	$113.0	$11,410	$400
26	$11,810	1.00%	$118.1	$11,928	$400
27	$12,328	1.00%	$123.3	$12,452	$400
28	$12,852	1.00%	$128.5	$12,980	$400
29	$13,380	1.00%	$133.8	$13,514	$400
30	$13,914	1.00%	$139.1	$14,053	$400
31	$14,453	1.00%	$144.5	$14,598	$400
32	$14,998	1.00%	$150.0	$15,148	$400
33	$15,548	1.00%	$155.5	$15,703	$400
34	$16,103	1.00%	$161.0	$16,264	$400
35	$16,664	1.00%	$166.6	$16,831	$400
36	$17,231	1.00%	$172.3	$17,403	$400

Number Of Contributions	Monthly Contribution	Monthly Return 12% ÷ 12	Interest Earned	Month End Total	Next Month Contribution
37	$17,803	1.00%	$178.0	$17,981	$400
38	$18,381	1.00%	$183.8	$18,565	$400
39	$18,965	1.00%	$189.6	$19,155	$400
40	$19,555	1.00%	$195.5	$19,750	$400
41	$20,150	1.00%	$201.5	$20,352	$400
42	$20,752	1.00%	$207.5	$20,959	$400
43	$21,359	1.00%	$213.6	$21,573	$400
44	$21,973	1.00%	$219.7	$22,192	$400
45	$22,592	1.00%	$225.9	$22,818	$400
46	$23,218	1.00%	$232.2	$23,451	$400
47	$23,851	1.00%	$238.5	$24,089	$400
48	$24,489	1.00%	$244.9	$24,734	$400
49	$25,134	1.00%	$251.3	$25,385	$400
50	$25,785	1.00%	$257.9	$26,043	$400
51	$26,443	1.00%	$264.4	$26,708	$400
52	$27,108	1.00%	$271.1	$27,379	$400
53	$27,779	1.00%	$277.8	$28,056	$400
54	$28,456	1.00%	$284.6	$28,741	$400
55	$29,141	1.00%	$291.4	$29,432	$400
56	$29,832	1.00%	$298.3	$30,131	$400
57	$30,531	1.00%	$305.3	$30,836	$400
58	$31,236	1.00%	$312.4	$31,548	$400
59	$31,948	1.00%	$319.5	$32,268	$400
60	$32,668	1.00%	$326.7	$32,995	$400
61	$33,395	1.00%	$333.9	$33,728	$400
62	$34,128	1.00%	$341.3	$34,470	$400
63	$34,870	1.00%	$348.7	$35,218	$400
64	$35,618	1.00%	$356.2	$35,975	$400
65	$36,375	1.00%	$363.7	$36,738	$400
66	$37,138	1.00%	$371.4	$37,510	$400
67	$37,910	1.00%	$379.1	$38,289	$400
68	$38,689	1.00%	$386.9	$39,076	$400
69	$39,476	1.00%	$394.8	$39,871	$400
70	$40,271	1.00%	$402.7	$40,673	$400
71	$41,073	1.00%	$410.7	$41,484	$400
72	$41,884	1.00%	$418.8	$42,303	$400
73	$42,703	1.00%	$427.0	$43,130	$400
74	$43,530	1.00%	$435.3	$43,965	$400
75	$44,365	1.00%	$443.7	$44,809	$400
76	$45,209	1.00%	$452.1	$45,661	$400

Number Of Contributions	Monthly Contribution	Monthly Return 12% ÷ 12	Interest Earned	Month End Total	Next Month Contribution
77	$46,061	1.00%	$460.6	$46,521	$400
78	$46,921	1.00%	$469.2	$47,391	$400
79	$47,791	1.00%	$477.9	$48,269	$400
80	$48,669	1.00%	$486.7	$49,155	$400
81	$49,555	1.00%	$495.6	$50,051	$400
82	$50,451	1.00%	$504.5	$50,955	$400
83	$51,355	1.00%	$513.6	$51,869	$400
84	$52,269	1.00%	$522.7	$52,792	$400
85	$53,192	1.00%	$531.9	$53,724	$400
86	$54,124	1.00%	$541.2	$54,665	$400
87	$55,065	1.00%	$550.6	$55,615	$400
88	$56,015	1.00%	$560.2	$56,576	$400
89	$56,976	1.00%	$569.8	$57,545	$400
90	$57,945	1.00%	$579.5	$58,525	$400
91	$58,925	1.00%	$589.2	$59,514	$400
92	$59,914	1.00%	$599.1	$60,513	$400
93	$60,913	1.00%	$609.1	$61,522	$400
94	$61,922	1.00%	$619.2	$62,542	$400
95	$62,942	1.00%	$629.4	$63,571	$400
96	$63,971	1.00%	$639.7	$64,611	$400
97	$65,011	1.00%	$650.1	$65,661	$400
98	$66,061	1.00%	$660.6	$66,721	$400
99	$67,121	1.00%	$671.2	$67,793	$400
100	$68,193	1.00%	$681.9	$68,874	$400
101	$69,274	1.00%	$692.7	$69,967	$400
102	$70,367	1.00%	$703.7	$71,071	$400
103	$71,471	1.00%	$714.7	$72,186	$400
104	$72,586	1.00%	$725.9	$73,311	$400
105	$73,711	1.00%	$737.1	$74,449	$400
106	$74,849	1.00%	$748.5	$75,597	$400
107	$75,997	1.00%	$760.0	$76,757	$400
108	$77,157	1.00%	$771.6	$77,929	$400
109	$78,329	1.00%	$783.3	$79,112	$400
110	$79,512	1.00%	$795.1	$80,307	$400
111	$80,707	1.00%	$807.1	$81,514	$400
112	$81,914	1.00%	$819.1	$82,733	$400
113	$83,133	1.00%	$831.3	$83,965	$400
114	$84,365	1.00%	$843.6	$85,208	$400
115	$85,608	1.00%	$856.1	$86,464	$400
116	$86,864	1.00%	$868.6	$87,733	$400

Number Of Contributions	Monthly Contribution	Monthly Return 12% ÷ 12	Interest Earned	Month End Total	Next Month Contribution
117	$88,133	1.00%	$881.3	$89,014	$400
118	$89,414	1.00%	$894.1	$90,308	$400
119	$90,708	1.00%	$907.1	$91,615	$400
120	$92,015	1.00%	$920.2	$92,936	$400
121	$93,336	1.00%	$933.4	$94,269	$400
122	$94,669	1.00%	$946.7	$95,616	$400
123	$96,016	1.00%	$960.2	$96,976	$400
124	$97,376	1.00%	$973.8	$98,350	$400
125	$98,750	1.00%	$987.5	$99,737	$400
126	$100,137	1.00%	$1,001.4	$101,138	$400
127	$101,538	1.00%	$1,015.4	$102,554	$400
128	$102,954	1.00%	$1,029.5	$103,983	$400
129	$104,383	1.00%	$1,043.8	$105,427	$400
130	$105,827	1.00%	$1,058.3	$106,885	$400
131	$107,285	1.00%	$1,072.9	$108,358	$400
132	$108,758	1.00%	$1,087.6	$109,846	$400
133	$110,246	1.00%	$1,102.5	$111,348	$400
134	$111,748	1.00%	$1,117.5	$112,866	$400
135	$113,266	1.00%	$1,132.7	$114,399	$400
136	$114,799	1.00%	$1,148.0	$115,947	$400
137	$116,347	1.00%	$1,163.5	$117,510	$400
138	$117,910	1.00%	$1,179.1	$119,089	$400
139	$119,489	1.00%	$1,194.9	$120,684	$400
140	$121,084	1.00%	$1,210.8	$122,295	$400
141	$122,695	1.00%	$1,226.9	$123,922	$400
142	$124,322	1.00%	$1,243.2	$125,565	$400
143	$125,965	1.00%	$1,259.6	$127,225	$400
144	$127,625	1.00%	$1,276.2	$128,901	$400
145	$129,301	1.00%	$1,293.0	$130,594	$400
146	$130,994	1.00%	$1,309.9	$132,304	$400
147	$132,704	1.00%	$1,327.0	$134,031	$400
148	$134,431	1.00%	$1,344.3	$135,775	$400
149	$136,175	1.00%	$1,361.8	$137,537	$400
150	$137,937	1.00%	$1,379.4	$139,316	$400
151	$139,716	1.00%	$1,397.2	$141,113	$400
152	$141,513	1.00%	$1,415.1	$142,929	$400
153	$143,329	1.00%	$1,433.3	$144,762	$400
154	$145,162	1.00%	$1,451.6	$146,613	$400
155	$147,013	1.00%	$1,470.1	$148,484	$400
156	$148,884	1.00%	$1,488.8	$150,372	$400

Number Of Contributions	Monthly Contribution	Monthly Return 12% ÷ 12	Interest Earned	Month End Total	Next Month Contribution
157	$150,772	1.00%	$1,507.7	$152,280	$400
158	$152,680	1.00%	$1,526.8	$154,207	$400
159	$154,607	1.00%	$1,546.1	$156,153	$400
160	$156,553	1.00%	$1,565.5	$158,119	$400
161	$158,519	1.00%	$1,585.2	$160,104	$400
162	$160,504	1.00%	$1,605.0	$162,109	$400
163	$162,509	1.00%	$1,625.1	$164,134	$400
164	$164,534	1.00%	$1,645.3	$166,179	$400
165	$166,579	1.00%	$1,665.8	$168,245	$400
166	$168,645	1.00%	$1,686.5	$170,331	$400
167	$170,731	1.00%	$1,707.3	$172,439	$400
168	$172,839	1.00%	$1,728.4	$174,567	$400
169	$174,967	1.00%	$1,749.7	$176,717	$400
170	$177,117	1.00%	$1,771.2	$178,888	$400
171	$179,288	1.00%	$1,792.9	$181,081	$400
172	$181,481	1.00%	$1,814.8	$183,296	$400
173	$183,696	1.00%	$1,837.0	$185,533	$400
174	$185,933	1.00%	$1,859.3	$187,792	$400
175	$188,192	1.00%	$1,881.9	$190,074	$400
176	$190,474	1.00%	$1,904.7	$192,379	$400
177	$192,779	1.00%	$1,927.8	$194,706	$400
178	$195,106	1.00%	$1,951.1	$197,058	$400
179	$197,458	1.00%	$1,974.6	$199,432	$400
180	$199,832	1.00%	$1,998.3	$201,830	$400
181	$202,230	1.00%	$2,022.3	$204,253	$400
182	$204,653	1.00%	$2,046.5	$206,699	$400
183	$207,099	1.00%	$2,071.0	$209,170	$400
184	$209,570	1.00%	$2,095.7	$211,666	$400
185	$212,066	1.00%	$2,120.7	$214,187	$400
186	$214,587	1.00%	$2,145.9	$216,732	$400
187	$217,132	1.00%	$2,171.3	$219,304	$400
188	$219,704	1.00%	$2,197.0	$221,901	$400
189	$222,301	1.00%	$2,223.0	$224,524	$400
190	$224,924	1.00%	$2,249.2	$227,173	$400
191	$227,573	1.00%	$2,275.7	$229,849	$400
192	$230,249	1.00%	$2,302.5	$232,551	$400
193	$232,951	1.00%	$2,329.5	$235,281	$400
194	$235,681	1.00%	$2,356.8	$238,038	$400
195	$238,438	1.00%	$2,384.4	$240,822	$400
196	$241,222	1.00%	$2,412.2	$243,634	$400

Number Of Contributions	Monthly Contribution	Monthly Return 12% ÷ 12	Interest Earned	Month End Total	Next Month Contribution
197	$244,034	1.00%	$2,440.3	$246,475	$400
198	$246,875	1.00%	$2,468.7	$249,343	$400
199	$249,743	1.00%	$2,497.4	$252,241	$400
200	$252,641	1.00%	$2,526.4	$255,167	$400
201	$255,567	1.00%	$2,555.7	$258,123	$400
202	$258,523	1.00%	$2,585.2	$261,108	$400
203	$261,508	1.00%	$2,615.1	$264,123	$400
204	$264,523	1.00%	$2,645.2	$267,168	$400
205	$267,568	1.00%	$2,675.7	$270,244	$400
206	$270,644	1.00%	$2,706.4	$273,350	$400
207	$273,750	1.00%	$2,737.5	$276,488	$400
208	$276,888	1.00%	$2,768.9	$279,657	$400
209	$280,057	1.00%	$2,800.6	$282,857	$400
210	$283,257	1.00%	$2,832.6	$286,090	$400
211	$286,490	1.00%	$2,864.9	$289,355	$400
212	$289,755	1.00%	$2,897.5	$292,652	$400
213	$293,052	1.00%	$2,930.5	$295,983	$400
214	$296,383	1.00%	$2,963.8	$299,347	$400
215	$299,747	1.00%	$2,997.5	$302,744	$400
216	$303,144	1.00%	$3,031.4	$306,176	$400
217	$306,576	1.00%	$3,065.8	$309,641	$400
218	$310,041	1.00%	$3,100.4	$313,142	$400
219	$313,542	1.00%	$3,135.4	$316,677	$400
220	$317,077	1.00%	$3,170.8	$320,248	$400
221	$320,648	1.00%	$3,206.5	$323,855	$400
222	$324,255	1.00%	$3,242.5	$327,497	$400
223	$327,897	1.00%	$3,279.0	$331,176	$400
224	$331,576	1.00%	$3,315.8	$334,892	$400
225	$335,292	1.00%	$3,352.9	$338,645	$400
226	$339,045	1.00%	$3,390.4	$342,435	$400
227	$342,835	1.00%	$3,428.4	$346,264	$400
228	$346,664	1.00%	$3,466.6	$350,130	$400
229	$350,530	1.00%	$3,505.3	$354,035	$400
230	$354,435	1.00%	$3,544.4	$357,980	$400
231	$358,380	1.00%	$3,583.8	$361,964	$400
232	$362,364	1.00%	$3,623.6	$365,987	$400
233	$366,387	1.00%	$3,663.9	$370,051	$400
234	$370,451	1.00%	$3,704.5	$374,156	$400
235	$374,556	1.00%	$3,745.6	$378,301	$400
236	$378,701	1.00%	$3,787.0	$382,488	$400

Number Of Contributions	Monthly Contribution	Monthly Return 12% ÷ 12	Interest Earned	Month End Total	Next Month Contribution
237	$382,888	1.00%	$3,828.9	$386,717	$400
238	$387,117	1.00%	$3,871.2	$390,988	$400
239	$391,388	1.00%	$3,913.9	$395,302	$400
240	$395,702	1.00%	$3,957.0	$399,659	$400
241	$400,059	1.00%	$4,000.6	$404,060	$400
242	$404,460	1.00%	$4,044.6	$408,504	$400
243	$408,904	1.00%	$4,089.0	$412,993	$400
244	$413,393	1.00%	$4,133.9	$417,527	$400
245	$417,927	1.00%	$4,179.3	$422,107	$400
246	$422,507	1.00%	$4,225.1	$426,732	$400
247	$427,132	1.00%	$4,271.3	$431,403	$400
248	$431,803	1.00%	$4,318.0	$436,121	$400
249	$436,521	1.00%	$4,365.2	$440,886	$400
250	$441,286	1.00%	$4,412.9	$445,699	$400
251	$446,099	1.00%	$4,461.0	$450,560	$400
252	$450,960	1.00%	$4,509.6	$455,470	$400
253	$455,870	1.00%	$4,558.7	$460,428	$400
254	$460,828	1.00%	$4,608.3	$465,437	$400
255	$465,837	1.00%	$4,658.4	$470,495	$400
256	$470,895	1.00%	$4,709.0	$475,604	$400
257	$476,004	1.00%	$4,760.0	$480,764	$400
258	$481,164	1.00%	$4,811.6	$485,976	$400
259	$486,376	1.00%	$4,863.8	$491,239	$400
260	$491,639	1.00%	$4,916.4	$496,556	$400
261	$496,956	1.00%	$4,969.6	$501,925	$400
262	$502,325	1.00%	$5,023.3	$507,349	$400
263	$507,749	1.00%	$5,077.5	$512,826	$400
264	$513,226	1.00%	$5,132.3	$518,358	$400
265	$518,758	1.00%	$5,187.6	$523,946	$400
266	$524,346	1.00%	$5,243.5	$529,589	$400
267	$529,989	1.00%	$5,299.9	$535,289	$400
268	$535,689	1.00%	$5,356.9	$541,046	$400
269	$541,446	1.00%	$5,414.5	$546,861	$400
270	$547,261	1.00%	$5,472.6	$552,733	$400
271	$553,133	1.00%	$5,531.3	$558,665	$400
272	$559,065	1.00%	$5,590.6	$564,655	$400
273	$565,055	1.00%	$5,650.6	$570,706	$400
274	$571,106	1.00%	$5,711.1	$576,817	$400
275	$577,217	1.00%	$5,772.2	$582,989	$400
276	$583,389	1.00%	$5,833.9	$589,223	$400

Number Of Contributions	Monthly Contribution	Monthly Return 12% ÷ 12	Interest Earned	Month End Total	Next Month Contribution
277	$589,623	1.00%	$5,896.2	$595,519	$400
278	$595,919	1.00%	$5,959.2	$601,878	$400
279	$602,278	1.00%	$6,022.8	$608,301	$400
280	$608,701	1.00%	$6,087.0	$614,788	$400
281	$615,188	1.00%	$6,151.9	$621,340	$400
282	$621,740	1.00%	$6,217.4	$627,957	$400
283	$628,357	1.00%	$6,283.6	$634,641	$400
284	$635,041	1.00%	$6,350.4	$641,391	$400
285	$641,791	1.00%	$6,417.9	$648,209	$400
286	$648,609	1.00%	$6,486.1	$655,095	$400
287	$655,495	1.00%	$6,555.0	$662,050	$400
288	$662,450	1.00%	$6,624.5	$669,075	$400
289	$669,475	1.00%	$6,694.7	$676,170	$400
290	$676,570	1.00%	$6,765.7	$683,335	$400
291	$683,735	1.00%	$6,837.4	$690,573	$400
292	$690,973	1.00%	$6,909.7	$697,882	$400
293	$698,282	1.00%	$6,982.8	$705,265	$400
294	$705,665	1.00%	$7,056.7	$712,722	$400
295	$713,122	1.00%	$7,131.2	$720,253	$400
296	$720,653	1.00%	$7,206.5	$727,860	$400
297	$728,260	1.00%	$7,282.6	$735,542	$400
298	$735,942	1.00%	$7,359.4	$743,302	$400
299	$743,702	1.00%	$7,437.0	$751,139	$400
300	$751,539	1.00%	$7,515.4	$759,054	$400
301	$759,454	1.00%	$7,594.5	$767,049	$400
302	$767,449	1.00%	$7,674.5	$775,123	$400
303	$775,523	1.00%	$7,755.2	$783,278	$400
304	$783,678	1.00%	$7,836.8	$791,515	$400
305	$791,915	1.00%	$7,919.2	$799,834	$400
306	$800,234	1.00%	$8,002.3	$808,237	$400
307	$808,637	1.00%	$8,086.4	$816,723	$400
308	$817,123	1.00%	$8,171.2	$825,294	$400
309	$825,694	1.00%	$8,256.9	$833,951	$400
310	$834,351	1.00%	$8,343.5	$842,695	$400
311	$843,095	1.00%	$8,430.9	$851,526	$400
312	$851,926	1.00%	$8,519.3	$860,445	$400
313	$860,845	1.00%	$8,608.4	$869,453	$400
314	$869,853	1.00%	$8,698.5	$878,552	$400
315	$878,952	1.00%	$8,789.5	$887,741	$400
316	$888,141	1.00%	$8,881.4	$897,023	$400

Number Of Contributions	Monthly Contribution	Monthly Return 12% ÷ 12	Interest Earned	Month End Total	Next Month Contribution
317	$897,423	1.00%	$8,974.2	$906,397	$400
318	$906,797	1.00%	$9,068.0	$915,865	$400
319	$916,265	1.00%	$9,162.6	$925,428	$400
320	$925,828	1.00%	$9,258.3	$935,086	$400
321	$935,486	1.00%	$9,354.9	$944,841	$400
322	$945,241	1.00%	$9,452.4	$954,693	$400
323	$955,093	1.00%	$9,550.9	$964,644	$400
324	$965,044	1.00%	$9,650.4	$974,694	$400
325	$975,094	1.00%	$9,750.9	$984,845	$400
326	$985,245	1.00%	$9,852.5	$995,098	$400
327	$995,498	1.00%	$9,955.0	$1,005,453	$400
328	$1,005,853	1.00%	$10,058.5	$1,015,911	$400
329	$1,016,311	1.00%	$10,163.1	$1,026,475	$400
330	$1,026,875	1.00%	$10,268.7	$1,037,143	$400
331	$1,037,543	1.00%	$10,375.4	$1,047,919	$400
332	$1,048,319	1.00%	$10,483.2	$1,058,802	$400
333	$1,059,202	1.00%	$10,592.0	$1,069,794	$400
334	$1,070,194	1.00%	$10,701.9	$1,080,896	$400
335	$1,081,296	1.00%	$10,813.0	$1,092,109	$400
336	$1,092,509	1.00%	$10,925.1	$1,103,434	$400
337	$1,103,834	1.00%	$11,038.3	$1,114,872	$400
338	$1,115,272	1.00%	$11,152.7	$1,126,425	$400
339	$1,126,825	1.00%	$11,268.2	$1,138,093	$400
340	$1,138,493	1.00%	$11,384.9	$1,149,878	$400
341	$1,150,278	1.00%	$11,502.8	$1,161,781	$400
342	$1,162,181	1.00%	$11,621.8	$1,173,803	$400
343	$1,174,203	1.00%	$11,742.0	$1,185,945	$400
344	$1,186,345	1.00%	$11,863.4	$1,198,208	$400
345	$1,198,608	1.00%	$11,986.1	$1,210,594	$400
346	$1,210,994	1.00%	$12,109.9	$1,223,104	$400
347	$1,223,504	1.00%	$12,235.0	$1,235,739	$400
348	$1,236,139	1.00%	$12,361.4	$1,248,501	$400
349	$1,248,901	1.00%	$12,489.0	$1,261,390	$400
350	$1,261,790	1.00%	$12,617.9	$1,274,408	$400
351	$1,274,808	1.00%	$12,748.1	$1,287,556	$400
352	$1,287,956	1.00%	$12,879.6	$1,300,835	$400
353	$1,301,235	1.00%	$13,012.4	$1,314,248	$400
354	$1,314,648	1.00%	$13,146.5	$1,327,794	$400
355	$1,328,194	1.00%	$13,281.9	$1,341,476	$400
356	$1,341,876	1.00%	$13,418.8	$1,355,295	$400

Number Of Contributions	Monthly Contribution	Monthly Return 12% ÷ 12	Interest Earned	Month End Total	Next Month Contribution
357	$1,355,695	1.00%	$13,556.9	$1,369,252	$400
358	$1,369,652	1.00%	$13,696.5	$1,383,348	$400
359	$1,383,748	1.00%	$13,837.5	$1,397,586	$400
360	$1,397,986	1.00%	$13,979.9	**$1,411,966**	

Appendix G (Chapter 22)
Starting Balance $40,000/$667 Month/30 years/8%

Number Of Contributions	Total Contribution	Monthly Return 8% ÷ 12	Interest Earned	Month End Total	Next Month Contribution
1	$40,667	0.67%	$272.5	$40,939	$667
2	$41,606	0.67%	$278.8	$41,885	$667
3	$42,552	0.67%	$285.1	$42,837	$667
4	$43,504	0.67%	$291.5	$43,796	$667
5	$44,463	0.67%	$297.9	$44,761	$667
6	$45,428	0.67%	$304.4	$45,732	$667
7	$46,399	0.67%	$310.9	$46,710	$667
8	$47,377	0.67%	$317.4	$47,694	$667
9	$48,361	0.67%	$324.0	$48,685	$667
10	$49,352	0.67%	$330.7	$49,683	$667
11	$50,350	0.67%	$337.3	$50,687	$667
12	$51,354	0.67%	$344.1	$51,698	$667
13	$52,365	0.67%	$350.8	$52,716	$667
14	$53,383	0.67%	$357.7	$53,741	$667
15	$54,408	0.67%	$364.5	$54,773	$667
16	$55,440	0.67%	$371.4	$55,811	$667
17	$56,478	0.67%	$378.4	$56,856	$667
18	$57,523	0.67%	$385.4	$57,909	$667
19	$58,576	0.67%	$392.5	$58,968	$667
20	$59,635	0.67%	$399.6	$60,035	$667
21	$60,702	0.67%	$406.7	$61,108	$667
22	$61,775	0.67%	$413.9	$62,189	$667
23	$62,856	0.67%	$421.1	$63,278	$667
24	$63,945	0.67%	$428.4	$64,373	$667
25	$65,040	0.67%	$435.8	$65,476	$667
26	$66,143	0.67%	$443.2	$66,586	$667
27	$67,253	0.67%	$450.6	$67,703	$667
28	$68,370	0.67%	$458.1	$68,829	$667
29	$69,496	0.67%	$465.6	$69,961	$667
30	$70,628	0.67%	$473.2	$71,101	$667
31	$71,768	0.67%	$480.8	$72,249	$667
32	$72,916	0.67%	$488.5	$73,405	$667
33	$74,072	0.67%	$496.3	$74,568	$667
34	$75,235	0.67%	$504.1	$75,739	$667
35	$76,406	0.67%	$511.9	$76,918	$667

Number Of Contributions	Total Contribution	Monthly Return 8% ÷ 12	Interest Earned	Month End Total	Next Month Contribution
36	$77,585	0.67%	$519.8	$78,105	$667
37	$78,772	0.67%	$527.8	$79,300	$667
38	$79,967	0.67%	$535.8	$80,502	$667
39	$81,169	0.67%	$543.8	$81,713	$667
40	$82,380	0.67%	$551.9	$82,932	$667
41	$83,599	0.67%	$560.1	$84,159	$667
42	$84,826	0.67%	$568.3	$85,395	$667
43	$86,062	0.67%	$576.6	$86,638	$667
44	$87,305	0.67%	$584.9	$87,890	$667
45	$88,557	0.67%	$593.3	$89,151	$667
46	$89,818	0.67%	$601.8	$90,419	$667
47	$91,086	0.67%	$610.3	$91,697	$667
48	$92,364	0.67%	$618.8	$92,982	$667
49	$93,649	0.67%	$627.5	$94,277	$667
50	$94,944	0.67%	$636.1	$95,580	$667
51	$96,247	0.67%	$644.9	$96,892	$667
52	$97,559	0.67%	$653.6	$98,213	$667
53	$98,880	0.67%	$662.5	$99,542	$667
54	$100,209	0.67%	$671.4	$100,880	$667
55	$101,547	0.67%	$680.4	$102,228	$667
56	$102,895	0.67%	$689.4	$103,584	$667
57	$104,251	0.67%	$698.5	$104,950	$667
58	$105,617	0.67%	$707.6	$106,324	$667
59	$106,991	0.67%	$716.8	$107,708	$667
60	$108,375	0.67%	$726.1	$109,101	$667
61	$109,768	0.67%	$735.4	$110,504	$667
62	$111,171	0.67%	$744.8	$111,916	$667
63	$112,583	0.67%	$754.3	$113,337	$667
64	$114,004	0.67%	$763.8	$114,768	$667
65	$115,435	0.67%	$773.4	$116,208	$667
66	$116,875	0.67%	$783.1	$117,658	$667
67	$118,325	0.67%	$792.8	$119,118	$667
68	$119,785	0.67%	$802.6	$120,587	$667
69	$121,254	0.67%	$812.4	$122,067	$667
70	$122,734	0.67%	$822.3	$123,556	$667
71	$124,223	0.67%	$832.3	$125,055	$667
72	$125,722	0.67%	$842.3	$126,565	$667
73	$127,232	0.67%	$852.5	$128,084	$667
74	$128,751	0.67%	$862.6	$129,614	$667

Number Of Contributions	Total Contribution	Monthly Return 8% ÷ 12	Interest Earned	Month End Total	Next Month Contribution
75	$130,281	0.67%	$872.9	$131,154	$667
76	$131,821	0.67%	$883.2	$132,704	$667
77	$133,371	0.67%	$893.6	$134,265	$667
78	$134,932	0.67%	$904.0	$135,836	$667
79	$136,503	0.67%	$914.6	$137,417	$667
80	$138,084	0.67%	$925.2	$139,009	$667
81	$139,676	0.67%	$935.8	$140,612	$667
82	$141,279	0.67%	$946.6	$142,226	$667
83	$142,893	0.67%	$957.4	$143,850	$667
84	$144,517	0.67%	$968.3	$145,485	$667
85	$146,152	0.67%	$979.2	$147,132	$667
86	$147,799	0.67%	$990.3	$148,789	$667
87	$149,456	0.67%	$1,001.4	$150,457	$667
88	$151,124	0.67%	$1,012.5	$152,137	$667
89	$152,804	0.67%	$1,023.8	$153,828	$667
90	$154,495	0.67%	$1,035.1	$155,530	$667
91	$156,197	0.67%	$1,046.5	$157,243	$667
92	$157,910	0.67%	$1,058.0	$158,968	$667
93	$159,635	0.67%	$1,069.6	$160,705	$667
94	$161,372	0.67%	$1,081.2	$162,453	$667
95	$163,120	0.67%	$1,092.9	$164,213	$667
96	$164,880	0.67%	$1,104.7	$165,985	$667
97	$166,652	0.67%	$1,116.6	$167,768	$667
98	$168,435	0.67%	$1,128.5	$169,564	$667
99	$170,231	0.67%	$1,140.5	$171,371	$667
100	$172,038	0.67%	$1,152.7	$173,191	$667
101	$173,858	0.67%	$1,164.8	$175,023	$667
102	$175,690	0.67%	$1,177.1	$176,867	$667
103	$177,534	0.67%	$1,189.5	$178,723	$667
104	$179,390	0.67%	$1,201.9	$180,592	$667
105	$181,259	0.67%	$1,214.4	$182,474	$667
106	$183,141	0.67%	$1,227.0	$184,368	$667
107	$185,035	0.67%	$1,239.7	$186,274	$667
108	$186,941	0.67%	$1,252.5	$188,194	$667
109	$188,861	0.67%	$1,265.4	$190,126	$667
110	$190,793	0.67%	$1,278.3	$192,072	$667
111	$192,739	0.67%	$1,291.3	$194,030	$667
112	$194,697	0.67%	$1,304.5	$196,001	$667
113	$196,668	0.67%	$1,317.7	$197,986	$667

Number Of Contributions	Total Contribution	Monthly Return 8% ÷ 12	Interest Earned	Month End Total	Next Month Contribution
114	$198,653	0.67%	$1,331.0	$199,984	$667
115	$200,651	0.67%	$1,344.4	$201,995	$667
116	$202,662	0.67%	$1,357.8	$204,020	$667
117	$204,687	0.67%	$1,371.4	$206,059	$667
118	$206,726	0.67%	$1,385.1	$208,111	$667
119	$208,778	0.67%	$1,398.8	$210,177	$667
120	$210,844	0.67%	$1,412.7	$212,256	$667
121	$212,923	0.67%	$1,426.6	$214,350	$667
122	$215,017	0.67%	$1,440.6	$216,457	$667
123	$217,124	0.67%	$1,454.7	$218,579	$667
124	$219,246	0.67%	$1,468.9	$220,715	$667
125	$221,382	0.67%	$1,483.3	$222,865	$667
126	$223,532	0.67%	$1,497.7	$225,030	$667
127	$225,697	0.67%	$1,512.2	$227,209	$667
128	$227,876	0.67%	$1,526.8	$229,403	$667
129	$230,070	0.67%	$1,541.5	$231,611	$667
130	$232,278	0.67%	$1,556.3	$233,835	$667
131	$234,502	0.67%	$1,571.2	$236,073	$667
132	$236,740	0.67%	$1,586.2	$238,326	$667
133	$238,993	0.67%	$1,601.3	$240,594	$667
134	$241,261	0.67%	$1,616.5	$242,878	$667
135	$243,545	0.67%	$1,631.7	$245,176	$667
136	$245,843	0.67%	$1,647.2	$247,491	$667
137	$248,158	0.67%	$1,662.7	$249,820	$667
138	$250,487	0.67%	$1,678.3	$252,165	$667
139	$252,832	0.67%	$1,694.0	$254,526	$667
140	$255,193	0.67%	$1,709.8	$256,903	$667
141	$257,570	0.67%	$1,725.7	$259,296	$667
142	$259,963	0.67%	$1,741.8	$261,705	$667
143	$262,372	0.67%	$1,757.9	$264,130	$667
144	$264,797	0.67%	$1,774.1	$266,571	$667
145	$267,238	0.67%	$1,790.5	$269,028	$667
146	$269,695	0.67%	$1,807.0	$271,502	$667
147	$272,169	0.67%	$1,823.5	$273,993	$667
148	$274,660	0.67%	$1,840.2	$276,500	$667
149	$277,167	0.67%	$1,857.0	$279,024	$667
150	$279,691	0.67%	$1,873.9	$281,565	$667
151	$282,232	0.67%	$1,891.0	$284,123	$667
152	$284,790	0.67%	$1,908.1	$286,698	$667

Number Of Contributions	Total Contribution	Monthly Return 8% ÷ 12	Interest Earned	Month End Total	Next Month Contribution
153	$287,365	0.67%	$1,925.3	$289,290	$667
154	$289,957	0.67%	$1,942.7	$291,900	$667
155	$292,567	0.67%	$1,960.2	$294,527	$667
156	$295,194	0.67%	$1,977.8	$297,172	$667
157	$297,839	0.67%	$1,995.5	$299,835	$667
158	$300,502	0.67%	$2,013.4	$302,515	$667
159	$303,182	0.67%	$2,031.3	$305,213	$667
160	$305,880	0.67%	$2,049.4	$307,930	$667
161	$308,597	0.67%	$2,067.6	$310,664	$667
162	$311,331	0.67%	$2,085.9	$313,417	$667
163	$314,084	0.67%	$2,104.4	$316,188	$667
164	$316,855	0.67%	$2,122.9	$318,978	$667
165	$319,645	0.67%	$2,141.6	$321,787	$667
166	$322,454	0.67%	$2,160.4	$324,614	$667
167	$325,281	0.67%	$2,179.4	$327,461	$667
168	$328,128	0.67%	$2,198.5	$330,326	$667
169	$330,993	0.67%	$2,217.7	$333,211	$667
170	$333,878	0.67%	$2,237.0	$336,115	$667
171	$336,782	0.67%	$2,256.4	$339,038	$667
172	$339,705	0.67%	$2,276.0	$341,981	$667
173	$342,648	0.67%	$2,295.7	$344,944	$667
174	$345,611	0.67%	$2,315.6	$347,927	$667
175	$348,594	0.67%	$2,335.6	$350,929	$667
176	$351,596	0.67%	$2,355.7	$353,952	$667
177	$354,619	0.67%	$2,375.9	$356,995	$667
178	$357,662	0.67%	$2,396.3	$360,058	$667
179	$360,725	0.67%	$2,416.9	$363,142	$667
180	$363,809	0.67%	$2,437.5	$366,247	$667
181	$366,914	0.67%	$2,458.3	$369,372	$667
182	$370,039	0.67%	$2,479.3	$372,518	$667
183	$373,185	0.67%	$2,500.3	$375,686	$667
184	$376,353	0.67%	$2,521.6	$378,874	$667
185	$379,541	0.67%	$2,542.9	$382,084	$667
186	$382,751	0.67%	$2,564.4	$385,316	$667
187	$385,983	0.67%	$2,586.1	$388,569	$667
188	$389,236	0.67%	$2,607.9	$391,844	$667
189	$392,511	0.67%	$2,629.8	$395,140	$667
190	$395,807	0.67%	$2,651.9	$398,459	$667
191	$399,126	0.67%	$2,674.1	$401,800	$667

Number Of Contributions	Total Contribution	Monthly Return 8% ÷ 12	Interest Earned	Month End Total	Next Month Contribution
192	$402,467	0.67%	$2,696.5	$405,164	$667
193	$405,831	0.67%	$2,719.1	$408,550	$667
194	$409,217	0.67%	$2,741.8	$411,959	$667
195	$412,626	0.67%	$2,764.6	$415,390	$667
196	$416,057	0.67%	$2,787.6	$418,845	$667
197	$419,512	0.67%	$2,810.7	$422,323	$667
198	$422,990	0.67%	$2,834.0	$425,824	$667
199	$426,491	0.67%	$2,857.5	$429,348	$667
200	$430,015	0.67%	$2,881.1	$432,896	$667
201	$433,563	0.67%	$2,904.9	$436,468	$667
202	$437,135	0.67%	$2,928.8	$440,064	$667
203	$440,731	0.67%	$2,952.9	$443,684	$667
204	$444,351	0.67%	$2,977.2	$447,328	$667
205	$447,995	0.67%	$3,001.6	$450,997	$667
206	$451,664	0.67%	$3,026.1	$454,690	$667
207	$455,357	0.67%	$3,050.9	$458,408	$667
208	$459,075	0.67%	$3,075.8	$462,150	$667
209	$462,817	0.67%	$3,100.9	$465,918	$667
210	$466,585	0.67%	$3,126.1	$469,711	$667
211	$470,378	0.67%	$3,151.5	$473,530	$667
212	$474,197	0.67%	$3,177.1	$477,374	$667
213	$478,041	0.67%	$3,202.9	$481,244	$667
214	$481,911	0.67%	$3,228.8	$485,140	$667
215	$485,807	0.67%	$3,254.9	$489,062	$667
216	$489,729	0.67%	$3,281.2	$493,010	$667
217	$493,677	0.67%	$3,307.6	$496,984	$667
218	$497,651	0.67%	$3,334.3	$500,986	$667
219	$501,653	0.67%	$3,361.1	$505,014	$667
220	$505,681	0.67%	$3,388.1	$509,069	$667
221	$509,736	0.67%	$3,415.2	$513,151	$667
222	$513,818	0.67%	$3,442.6	$517,261	$667
223	$517,928	0.67%	$3,470.1	$521,398	$667
224	$522,065	0.67%	$3,497.8	$525,563	$667
225	$526,230	0.67%	$3,525.7	$529,755	$667
226	$530,422	0.67%	$3,553.8	$533,976	$667
227	$534,643	0.67%	$3,582.1	$538,225	$667
228	$538,892	0.67%	$3,610.6	$542,503	$667
229	$543,170	0.67%	$3,639.2	$546,809	$667
230	$547,476	0.67%	$3,668.1	$551,144	$667

Number Of Contributions	Total Contribution	Monthly Return 8% ÷ 12	Interest Earned	Month End Total	Next Month Contribution
231	$551,811	0.67%	$3,697.1	$555,508	$667
232	$556,175	0.67%	$3,726.4	$559,902	$667
233	$560,569	0.67%	$3,755.8	$564,325	$667
234	$564,992	0.67%	$3,785.4	$568,777	$667
235	$569,444	0.67%	$3,815.3	$573,259	$667
236	$573,926	0.67%	$3,845.3	$577,772	$667
237	$578,439	0.67%	$3,875.5	$582,314	$667
238	$582,981	0.67%	$3,906.0	$586,887	$667
239	$587,554	0.67%	$3,936.6	$591,491	$667
240	$592,158	0.67%	$3,967.5	**$596,125**	

Appendix H (Chapter 22)
Starting Balance $40,000/$667 Month/30 years/12%

Number Of Contributions	Monthly Contribution	Monthly Return 12% ÷ 12	Interest Earned	Month End Total	Next Month Contribution
1	$40,667	1.00%	$406.7	$41,074	$667
2	$41,741	1.00%	$417.4	$42,158	$667
3	$42,825	1.00%	$428.3	$43,253	$667
4	$43,920	1.00%	$439.2	$44,360	$667
5	$45,027	1.00%	$450.3	$45,477	$667
6	$46,144	1.00%	$461.4	$46,605	$667
7	$47,272	1.00%	$472.7	$47,745	$667
8	$48,412	1.00%	$484.1	$48,896	$667
9	$49,563	1.00%	$495.6	$50,059	$667
10	$50,726	1.00%	$507.3	$51,233	$667
11	$51,900	1.00%	$519.0	$52,419	$667
12	$53,086	1.00%	$530.9	$53,617	$667
13	$54,284	1.00%	$542.8	$54,827	$667
14	$55,494	1.00%	$554.9	$56,049	$667
15	$56,716	1.00%	$567.2	$57,283	$667
16	$57,950	1.00%	$579.5	$58,529	$667
17	$59,196	1.00%	$592.0	$59,788	$667
18	$60,455	1.00%	$604.6	$61,060	$667
19	$61,727	1.00%	$617.3	$62,344	$667
20	$63,011	1.00%	$630.1	$63,641	$667
21	$64,308	1.00%	$643.1	$64,951	$667
22	$65,618	1.00%	$656.2	$66,274	$667
23	$66,941	1.00%	$669.4	$67,611	$667
24	$68,278	1.00%	$682.8	$68,961	$667
25	$69,628	1.00%	$696.3	$70,324	$667
26	$70,991	1.00%	$709.9	$71,701	$667
27	$72,368	1.00%	$723.7	$73,091	$667
28	$73,758	1.00%	$737.6	$74,496	$667
29	$75,163	1.00%	$751.6	$75,915	$667
30	$76,582	1.00%	$765.8	$77,347	$667
31	$78,014	1.00%	$780.1	$78,795	$667
32	$79,462	1.00%	$794.6	$80,256	$667
33	$80,923	1.00%	$809.2	$81,732	$667
34	$82,399	1.00%	$824.0	$83,223	$667
35	$83,890	1.00%	$838.9	$84,729	$667

Number Of Contributions	Monthly Contribution	Monthly Return 12% ÷ 12	Interest Earned	Month End Total	Next Month Contribution
36	$85,396	1.00%	$854.0	$86,250	$667
37	$86,917	1.00%	$869.2	$87,787	$667
38	$88,454	1.00%	$884.5	$89,338	$667
39	$90,005	1.00%	$900.1	$90,905	$667
40	$91,572	1.00%	$915.7	$92,488	$667
41	$93,155	1.00%	$931.5	$94,086	$667
42	$94,753	1.00%	$947.5	$95,701	$667
43	$96,368	1.00%	$963.7	$97,332	$667
44	$97,999	1.00%	$980.0	$98,979	$667
45	$99,646	1.00%	$996.5	$100,642	$667
46	$101,309	1.00%	$1,013.1	$102,322	$667
47	$102,989	1.00%	$1,029.9	$104,019	$667
48	$104,686	1.00%	$1,046.9	$105,733	$667
49	$106,400	1.00%	$1,064.0	$107,464	$667
50	$108,131	1.00%	$1,081.3	$109,212	$667
51	$109,879	1.00%	$1,098.8	$110,978	$667
52	$111,645	1.00%	$1,116.4	$112,761	$667
53	$113,428	1.00%	$1,134.3	$114,563	$667
54	$115,230	1.00%	$1,152.3	$116,382	$667
55	$117,049	1.00%	$1,170.5	$118,219	$667
56	$118,886	1.00%	$1,188.9	$120,075	$667
57	$120,742	1.00%	$1,207.4	$121,950	$667
58	$122,617	1.00%	$1,226.2	$123,843	$667
59	$124,510	1.00%	$1,245.1	$125,755	$667
60	$126,422	1.00%	$1,264.2	$127,686	$667
61	$128,353	1.00%	$1,283.5	$129,637	$667
62	$130,304	1.00%	$1,303.0	$131,607	$667
63	$132,274	1.00%	$1,322.7	$133,597	$667
64	$134,264	1.00%	$1,342.6	$135,606	$667
65	$136,273	1.00%	$1,362.7	$137,636	$667
66	$138,303	1.00%	$1,383.0	$139,686	$667
67	$140,353	1.00%	$1,403.5	$141,757	$667
68	$142,424	1.00%	$1,424.2	$143,848	$667
69	$144,515	1.00%	$1,445.1	$145,960	$667
70	$146,627	1.00%	$1,466.3	$148,093	$667
71	$148,760	1.00%	$1,487.6	$150,248	$667
72	$150,915	1.00%	$1,509.1	$152,424	$667
73	$153,091	1.00%	$1,530.9	$154,622	$667
74	$155,289	1.00%	$1,552.9	$156,842	$667

Number Of Contributions	Monthly Contribution	Monthly Return 12% ÷ 12	Interest Earned	Month End Total	Next Month Contribution
75	$157,509	1.00%	$1,575.1	$159,084	$667
76	$159,751	1.00%	$1,597.5	$161,348	$667
77	$162,015	1.00%	$1,620.2	$163,635	$667
78	$164,302	1.00%	$1,643.0	$165,945	$667
79	$166,612	1.00%	$1,666.1	$168,279	$667
80	$168,946	1.00%	$1,689.5	$170,635	$667
81	$171,302	1.00%	$1,713.0	$173,015	$667
82	$173,682	1.00%	$1,736.8	$175,419	$667
83	$176,086	1.00%	$1,760.9	$177,847	$667
84	$178,514	1.00%	$1,785.1	$180,299	$667
85	$180,966	1.00%	$1,809.7	$182,776	$667
86	$183,443	1.00%	$1,834.4	$185,277	$667
87	$185,944	1.00%	$1,859.4	$187,803	$667
88	$188,470	1.00%	$1,884.7	$190,355	$667
89	$191,022	1.00%	$1,910.2	$192,932	$667
90	$193,599	1.00%	$1,936.0	$195,535	$667
91	$196,202	1.00%	$1,962.0	$198,164	$667
92	$198,831	1.00%	$1,988.3	$200,820	$667
93	$201,487	1.00%	$2,014.9	$203,502	$667
94	$204,169	1.00%	$2,041.7	$206,210	$667
95	$206,877	1.00%	$2,068.8	$208,946	$667
96	$209,613	1.00%	$2,096.1	$211,709	$667
97	$212,376	1.00%	$2,123.8	$214,500	$667
98	$215,167	1.00%	$2,151.7	$217,319	$667
99	$217,986	1.00%	$2,179.9	$220,165	$667
100	$220,832	1.00%	$2,208.3	$223,041	$667
101	$223,708	1.00%	$2,237.1	$225,945	$667
102	$226,612	1.00%	$2,266.1	$228,878	$667
103	$229,545	1.00%	$2,295.4	$231,840	$667
104	$232,507	1.00%	$2,325.1	$234,832	$667
105	$235,499	1.00%	$2,355.0	$237,854	$667
106	$238,521	1.00%	$2,385.2	$240,907	$667
107	$241,574	1.00%	$2,415.7	$243,989	$667
108	$244,656	1.00%	$2,446.6	$247,103	$667
109	$247,770	1.00%	$2,477.7	$250,248	$667
110	$250,915	1.00%	$2,509.1	$253,424	$667
111	$254,091	1.00%	$2,540.9	$256,632	$667
112	$257,299	1.00%	$2,573.0	$259,872	$667
113	$260,539	1.00%	$2,605.4	$263,144	$667

Number Of Contributions	Monthly Contribution	Monthly Return 12% ÷ 12	Interest Earned	Month End Total	Next Month Contribution
114	$263,811	1.00%	$2,638.1	$266,449	$667
115	$267,116	1.00%	$2,671.2	$269,787	$667
116	$270,454	1.00%	$2,704.5	$273,159	$667
117	$273,826	1.00%	$2,738.3	$276,564	$667
118	$277,231	1.00%	$2,772.3	$280,003	$667
119	$280,670	1.00%	$2,806.7	$283,477	$667
120	$284,144	1.00%	$2,841.4	$286,986	$667
121	$287,653	1.00%	$2,876.5	$290,529	$667
122	$291,196	1.00%	$2,912.0	$294,108	$667
123	$294,775	1.00%	$2,947.8	$297,723	$667
124	$298,390	1.00%	$2,983.9	$301,374	$667
125	$302,041	1.00%	$3,020.4	$305,061	$667
126	$305,728	1.00%	$3,057.3	$308,785	$667
127	$309,452	1.00%	$3,094.5	$312,547	$667
128	$313,214	1.00%	$3,132.1	$316,346	$667
129	$317,013	1.00%	$3,170.1	$320,183	$667
130	$320,850	1.00%	$3,208.5	$324,059	$667
131	$324,726	1.00%	$3,247.3	$327,973	$667
132	$328,640	1.00%	$3,286.4	$331,926	$667
133	$332,593	1.00%	$3,325.9	$335,919	$667
134	$336,586	1.00%	$3,365.9	$339,952	$667
135	$340,619	1.00%	$3,406.2	$344,025	$667
136	$344,692	1.00%	$3,446.9	$348,139	$667
137	$348,806	1.00%	$3,488.1	$352,294	$667
138	$352,961	1.00%	$3,529.6	$356,491	$667
139	$357,158	1.00%	$3,571.6	$360,730	$667
140	$361,397	1.00%	$3,614.0	$365,011	$667
141	$365,678	1.00%	$3,656.8	$369,334	$667
142	$370,001	1.00%	$3,700.0	$373,701	$667
143	$374,368	1.00%	$3,743.7	$378,112	$667
144	$378,779	1.00%	$3,787.8	$382,567	$667
145	$383,234	1.00%	$3,832.3	$387,066	$667
146	$387,733	1.00%	$3,877.3	$391,610	$667
147	$392,277	1.00%	$3,922.8	$396,200	$667
148	$396,867	1.00%	$3,968.7	$400,836	$667
149	$401,503	1.00%	$4,015.0	$405,518	$667
150	$406,185	1.00%	$4,061.8	$410,247	$667
151	$410,914	1.00%	$4,109.1	$415,023	$667
152	$415,690	1.00%	$4,156.9	$419,847	$667

Number Of Contributions	Monthly Contribution	Monthly Return 12% ÷ 12	Interest Earned	Month End Total	Next Month Contribution
153	$420,514	1.00%	$4,205.1	$424,719	$667
154	$425,386	1.00%	$4,253.9	$429,640	$667
155	$430,307	1.00%	$4,303.1	$434,610	$667
156	$435,277	1.00%	$4,352.8	$439,630	$667
157	$440,297	1.00%	$4,403.0	$444,700	$667
158	$445,367	1.00%	$4,453.7	$449,820	$667
159	$450,487	1.00%	$4,504.9	$454,992	$667
160	$455,659	1.00%	$4,556.6	$460,216	$667
161	$460,883	1.00%	$4,608.8	$465,492	$667
162	$466,159	1.00%	$4,661.6	$470,820	$667
163	$471,487	1.00%	$4,714.9	$476,202	$667
164	$476,869	1.00%	$4,768.7	$481,638	$667
165	$482,305	1.00%	$4,823.0	$487,128	$667
166	$487,795	1.00%	$4,877.9	$492,673	$667
167	$493,340	1.00%	$4,933.4	$498,273	$667
168	$498,940	1.00%	$4,989.4	$503,930	$667
169	$504,597	1.00%	$5,046.0	$509,643	$667
170	$510,310	1.00%	$5,103.1	$515,413	$667
171	$516,080	1.00%	$5,160.8	$521,240	$667
172	$521,907	1.00%	$5,219.1	$527,126	$667
173	$527,793	1.00%	$5,277.9	$533,071	$667
174	$533,738	1.00%	$5,337.4	$539,076	$667
175	$539,743	1.00%	$5,397.4	$545,140	$667
176	$545,807	1.00%	$5,458.1	$551,265	$667
177	$551,932	1.00%	$5,519.3	$557,452	$667
178	$558,119	1.00%	$5,581.2	$563,700	$667
179	$564,367	1.00%	$5,643.7	$570,010	$667
180	$570,677	1.00%	$5,706.8	$576,384	$667
181	$577,051	1.00%	$5,770.5	$582,822	$667
182	$583,489	1.00%	$5,834.9	$589,324	$667
183	$589,991	1.00%	$5,899.9	$595,891	$667
184	$596,558	1.00%	$5,965.6	$602,523	$667
185	$603,190	1.00%	$6,031.9	$609,222	$667
186	$609,889	1.00%	$6,098.9	$615,988	$667
187	$616,655	1.00%	$6,166.5	$622,821	$667
188	$623,488	1.00%	$6,234.9	$629,723	$667
189	$630,390	1.00%	$6,303.9	$636,694	$667
190	$637,361	1.00%	$6,373.6	$643,735	$667
191	$644,402	1.00%	$6,444.0	$650,846	$667

Number Of Contributions	Monthly Contribution	Monthly Return 12% ÷ 12	Interest Earned	Month End Total	Next Month Contribution
192	$651,513	1.00%	$6,515.1	$658,028	$667
193	$658,695	1.00%	$6,587.0	$665,282	$667
194	$665,949	1.00%	$6,659.5	$672,608	$667
195	$673,275	1.00%	$6,732.8	$680,008	$667
196	$680,675	1.00%	$6,806.8	$687,482	$667
197	$688,149	1.00%	$6,881.5	$695,030	$667
198	$695,697	1.00%	$6,957.0	$702,654	$667
199	$703,321	1.00%	$7,033.2	$710,355	$667
200	$711,022	1.00%	$7,110.2	$718,132	$667
201	$718,799	1.00%	$7,188.0	$725,987	$667
202	$726,654	1.00%	$7,266.5	$733,920	$667
203	$734,587	1.00%	$7,345.9	$741,933	$667
204	$742,600	1.00%	$7,426.0	$750,026	$667
205	$750,693	1.00%	$7,506.9	$758,200	$667
206	$758,867	1.00%	$7,588.7	$766,456	$667
207	$767,123	1.00%	$7,671.2	$774,794	$667
208	$775,461	1.00%	$7,754.6	$783,216	$667
209	$783,883	1.00%	$7,838.8	$791,722	$667
210	$792,389	1.00%	$7,923.9	$800,312	$667
211	$800,979	1.00%	$8,009.8	$808,989	$667
212	$809,656	1.00%	$8,096.6	$817,753	$667
213	$818,420	1.00%	$8,184.2	$826,604	$667
214	$827,271	1.00%	$8,272.7	$835,544	$667
215	$836,211	1.00%	$8,362.1	$844,573	$667
216	$845,240	1.00%	$8,452.4	$853,692	$667
217	$854,359	1.00%	$8,543.6	$862,903	$667
218	$863,570	1.00%	$8,635.7	$872,206	$667
219	$872,873	1.00%	$8,728.7	$881,601	$667
220	$882,268	1.00%	$8,822.7	$891,091	$667
221	$891,758	1.00%	$8,917.6	$900,675	$667
222	$901,342	1.00%	$9,013.4	$910,356	$667
223	$911,023	1.00%	$9,110.2	$920,133	$667
224	$920,800	1.00%	$9,208.0	$930,008	$667
225	$930,675	1.00%	$9,306.8	$939,982	$667
226	$940,649	1.00%	$9,406.5	$950,055	$667
227	$950,722	1.00%	$9,507.2	$960,230	$667
228	$960,897	1.00%	$9,609.0	$970,506	$667
229	$971,173	1.00%	$9,711.7	$980,884	$667
230	$981,551	1.00%	$9,815.5	$991,367	$667

Number Of Contributions	Monthly Contribution	Monthly Return 12% ÷ 12	Interest Earned	Month End Total	Next Month Contribution
231	$992,034	1.00%	$9,920.3	$1,001,954	$667
232	$1,002,621	1.00%	$10,026.2	$1,012,647	$667
233	$1,013,314	1.00%	$10,133.1	$1,023,448	$667
234	$1,024,115	1.00%	$10,241.1	$1,034,356	$667
235	$1,035,023	1.00%	$10,350.2	$1,045,373	$667
236	$1,046,040	1.00%	$10,460.4	$1,056,500	$667
237	$1,057,167	1.00%	$10,571.7	$1,067,739	$667
238	$1,068,406	1.00%	$10,684.1	$1,079,090	$667
239	$1,079,757	1.00%	$10,797.6	$1,090,555	$667
240	$1,091,222	1.00%	$10,912.2	**$1,102,134**	

www.ingramcontent.com/pod-product-compliance
Lightning Source LLC
Chambersburg PA
CBHW030920180526
45163CB00002B/404